117783

D1554561

PRACTICAL TRUTHS
FROM
JONAH

by
Joseph S. Exell

PRACTICAL TRUTHS
FROM
JONAH

by
Joseph S. Exell

KREGEL PUBLICATIONS
Grand Rapids, Michigan 49501

Library of Congress Cataloging in Publication Data

Exell, Joseph S. (Joseph Samuel), 1849-1909.
 Practical Truths from Jonah.

 Reprint. Originally published: Practical readings
in the Book of Jonah. London : Elliot Stock, 1874.
 1. Bible. O.T. Jonah—Criticism, interpretation,
etc. I. Title.
BS1605.2.E83   1982   224'.9206   82-18671
ISBN 0-8254-2525-5

Printed in the United States of America

CONTENTS

PUBLISHER'S PREFACE

Exell's remarkable ability to pinpoint proper applications is the element that makes this commentary unique. His ability comes from a love for God and a proper understanding of the historical, cultural, grammatical context.

His style is verse-by-verse, making several relevant comments on each verse. It is not intended to be an exhaustive commentary, rather a suggestive one. Each verse offers several fresh thoughts and insights, designed to bring every reader into a deeper knowledge of God, His loving judgments and His matchless grace.

The scholarly magazine of the past, the "Homilist" stated well the purpose of Joseph S. Exell: "His object is to reach and raise into light the great practical truths that run through the book, and this he has done with singular success."

The publishers take great pleasure in releasing *Practical Truths From Jonah*. It will challenge your thinking and move your heart.

The Publishers

JONAH 1

NOW numerous are the voices which discourse to the soul. Nature ever holds converse with appreciative listeners. Her grandeur speaks of God; her beauty of moral perfection; while her periods of decay and growth teach the sad, but hopeful meaning of human life. And, hearing this voice, our spirits have been thrilled by its eloquence, and our lives enriched by its instruction. Also, everyday occurrences speak to us; warning of evil by the wreck of its hope, attracting to virtue by the purity of its triumph. But there are times in life when God closes the avenues of our being to every presence but His Own. Then, taken from the unrest of toil, lifted into higher experiences; the soul, bathed in celestial calm, is opened to the dawning visions of another world. Such times, though measured by the clock as hours, are truly divine eras, wherein, in a moment, we live the deep life of a century. Such was the case with Jonah.

Look at the nature of this communication. It was *audible*. "The *word* of the Lord." In the early dawn of truth, man's æsthetic nature was made the medium of heavenly intercourse. Now spiritual impressions have taken the place of vocal utterances. True manhood is always sensitive to the finger of God; at points unknown; at times unlikely; in places most inconceivable He comes; and, hovering quietly over, breathes upon the trembling spirit an intuitive consciousness of duty. It was also *definite*: not filling the mind of Jonah with vague impression, or uncertain doubt, giving but a faint revelation of events augurial. The message, clear to his intellect, took deep hold of his consciousness, as the sequel of the narrative proves. True, the meaning of such tidings has not always been comprehended. This we could not naturally expect. There are in the Divine existence, oceans of emotion, empires of thought, and such unknown qualities, for the mention of which we have no name, that language could not convey, nor human perception understand their magnitude. The communication was *brief*. There was no introduction; no empty rhetoric, no display of heavenly effulgence; but a laconic expression of will. Communion with God does not necessarily hold us long; a moment is enough, in a syllable He can utter thoughts, and expound principles, the meaning of which a life time will not unfold.

The communications of God are *human in their destiny*. "Unto Jonah." The selections of life are Divine; not arbitrary, but according to the deepest law of requirement. Not merely the city to be taught, but also the moral condition of the individual to be sent, determine the choice; that the legation may be disciplinary to both. The soul-life of Jonah would be intensified by this embassy. Tempest might threaten disaster, whereas in reality it would remove the artificial elements of his character, and impart the germs of a larger manhood. Many people grow restless because they are not preferred for the great duties of life ; forgetting that all cannot be chosen, and that, though honourable, these charges are responsible; bringing into a publicity from which you cannot retire, and which will but augment the chagrin of failure. Hence, God having more respect for you than to permit this, detains in the peaceful solitude of unknown toil. The lovely color of the wild flower, sheltered by the mountain crags, might fade into decay if transplanted to the general thoroughfare. Thus, instead of distrust, the considerateness of Divine Providence should inspire, not merely tranquility, but gratitude. Here we find that *God influences man by man.* The commission came to Jonah, not to an angel ; not to a Hermit in the woods, or a Recluse in the cloister, but to the *son* of Amittai. These are heart words, intensely pathetic ; appealing to the higher feelings of our nature. It seems as if the Divine Being wished to remove the awfulness of His command by the toning influence of domestic life. True, to be efficient, man must be God-sent, yet he must also be qualified by fervent human sympathies. The icy officialism of the Prophet, should be tempered into gentleness by the warmth of a filial kinship : who so likely to attract a mother's heart, to influence a rebellious child, or to reclaim a degenerate city, as the *son* of Amittai.

Arise, go to Nineveh, that great city, and cry against it ; for their wickedness is come up before me.—*Ver.* 2.

Divine messages require immediate attention. When

God speaks He has something to communicate ; hence
it becomes man to listen carefully, and obey diligently.
He enjoins the abeyance of all personal considerations.
Jonah is now in an especial degree the property of
another. His social, civil, and commercial duties must
yield to the dictum of a higher authority. True, he
would have been far more comfortable in the unten-
sion of home, than in the restraint of a foreign city ;
more happy at his everyday toil, than in preaching to
the demoralized crowds of Nineveh. But when the
Divine Voice utters its sovereign behest, all thoughts
of home must vanish like dreams of night at the break
of morning. However turbulent the heart with unuttered feeling, it must immediately fall into an obedient
calm. Such discipline is frequently required. The
widow's son is consigned to a foreign country ; conscience demands obedience ; separation appears inevitable. The mother weeps, the youth trembles, but
hearing the voice, "Arise," they yield to its injunction.

We require deeper penetration to see, beneath apparent hardships, the Divine motive of love. In order
to this self-conquest, powerful effort is requisite. Not
merely a quiescent drifting of the mind, but concen-
trated work. "*Arise*"—shake off the inherent dila-
toriness of human nature ; awake from the stupor of
past unfaithfulness ; summon energy to its highest
point of action, until tremor is lost in the certitude of
habit. Then the mission, becoming the natural element
of life, will be hopefully achieved.

Thus we learn that *Divine communications often
enjoin a melancholy and arduous duty.* Jonah was
sent to cry against Nineveh ! A journey, long, and

unexpeditious. He was sent to a foreign city; indicating that the spiritual is diviner than the national. Beneath the Gentile lay the man; universal; one in the grief of a sinful nature, in the restlessness of mortified hope, and possibly in the trust of a calmer hope upon the ideal manhood of life. Christ is the resting point of national oneness; the march of every true kingdom is toward Him. Nineveh was a *great city*. Its noble buildings, gleaming in the sunshine, reflected their lofty turrets in the waters of the Tigris. Its wealth was uncalculated, its resources illimitable, and its luxury epicurean. Walking its streets are merchants frantic with commercial speculation; here pursuing errands of passion, there devising cunning theft, by which to enrich unholy greed. The general rush of the city is onward; onward to a destiny whose awfulness only volcanic language could articulate. With this sweep of degenerate life Jonah was to mingle, not to imbibe its pollution, but to roll back its current. Upon the almost lifeless, seething heap of corruption, he was either to reflect a sunbeam to cheer, or lightning to destroy. Deeply would Jonah feel the responsibility and difficulty of the task. But if the prophet was weak, God was strong; if the city was great, God was greater. How imagination would sketch the picture, touched into awfulness by the pencillings of fear. Alone, in such a city, with so terrible a message. Jonah, no doubt lived mentally in Nineveh long before he went; and frequently would his reveries be agitated by the clamour of a mythical crowd. Then his earnest demeanour would incur misrepresentation, and excite irony. He was to *cry* against the city. Not reforming

it by private effort, working from the individual to the
mass; but by an open attack from the very commencement of his residence therein. He was to throw
all the enthusiasm of his being into the mission.
Many people cannot *cry;* they have not force of
soul; they are not endowed for extreme effort. Impulse never carries beyond themselves. It never rises
to inspiration, leading to spontaneous, unconventional
self-abandonment. It is not deemed orthodox to cry;
hence the feeble spirit just mutters its anathemas
against the wrong. While others, having the requisite
power of character, resenting energetically personal
injury, hear without reproof a disrespectful mention of
God. Is it so with us? We have our wicked Nine-
vehs. That city with its drunkenness, profligacy, murder, and deception. Do we cry against it? or pass
gently on the other side, afraid of contamination;
hastening on, lest anyone watching should suspect
complicity, with unspoken disgust. Oh! that we felt
more deeply on this matter. Talk of avoiding evil
because its shadow may fall upon you! The purity
of your life should elevate above suspicion. The sunbeam falls upon murky towers, penetrates the smokiest
atmosphere, and gleams through the broken shutters
of the poorest hut; yet no one associates its glory with
the surrounding corruption. The opposite is true; contrast makes its lustre more apparent. If our piety
were thus vigorous, and beautiful, the finger of character
might touch the darkest life, at its midnight point,
without apprehension. Try then to diminish municipal
sin, to let in upon its impurity the light of the Cross,
to hush its passion by the voice Divine, to remove its

tears by striking into its deepest being the harmony of
another world. Jonah was not misled as to the difficulty
of his mission. God informed him that the city was great,
that its character was unholy. He never takes advantage of human nature; surprising its infirmity or
indulging its fear, but fortifies by a communication of
hardship.

Divine communications are frequently *occasioned by
human sinfulness.* " For their wickedness is come up
before me." This would tell Jonah that he could have
no hope of safety in the moral character of the city; no
doubt, murder was already in the catalogue of its felony.
Does not this teach us the effrontery of human nature,
and the righteous indignation of God thereon ? Also,
that *collective sin does not escape the notice of heaven ?*
Men strive to fasten themselves in the great bundle of
life, that their personality may be merged in the company
of others. How many corporations act as though
totally destitute of responsibility ? When injustice is
advocated, silence is consentient, and only protesta-
tion can avert reproach. True, our conduct may be
hid from others; from our constituency, from our neigh-
bours; but not from God. He hears the unspoken
inclination of the soul, likewise the verbosities of the
lip; computes the total, and mysteriously, but unerringly, allots a degree of liability in the same ratio as
each contributed to the issue. As God not only beholds
the globe, rolling in the immensity of space at his
feet, but also every flower opening into blossom, or
falling to decay: so He is equally cognizant of
personal character. The mute passion of the heart,
the besetment of the life, the blasphemy of every oath,

the impurity of every companionship, is as naked to Him as the entirety of human wickedness. But the sin of the Ninevites did not require Omniscience to penetrate its depths; its magnitude was such that it came unbidden into the Divine Presence. They threw down the gauntlet before God, and openly invited Him to conflict.

But Jonah rose up to flee unto Tarshish from the presence of the Lord, and went down to Joppa; and he found a ship going to Tarshish : so he paid the fare thereof, and went down into it, to go with them unto Tarshish from the presence of the Lord.—*Ver.* **3.**

This verse teaches *the possibilities of human nature* —showing both its strength and weakness. The former, in that it can resist God; the latter, in that it does. Weakness is never so generally manifested as in the use of power. Men appear unable to wield the rod of Empire with steady grasp. Its tenure evokes pride, excites ambition, and often merges gentleness in the rebuff of tyranny. Equally impotent is self-rule : thought becomes vagrant, passion dictatorial, and manhood yields supremacy to inclination. Jonah's weakness did not consist in the petulance of the Despot, but in the recoil of cowardice. Look at his *folly.* "He rose up to flee to Tarshish." Why did he select this town ? Had he friends there ? Was it at an extreme point from Nineveh ? Or was he influenced by the casual readiness of the ship ? We cannot tell; but could he not with equal facility have gone to Nineveh ? The energy aroused; its streams might as easily have flown in the right channel as the wrong.

Who can estimate *the waste of soul power that there is in human life ?* This is illustrated in the conduct

of Jonah ? What anxious thought, regretting precaution, and bitter suspense, would he endure on this
voyage to Tarshish. It must have taken no ordinary
will-power to have quelled the storm within him, that
others might not become cognizant of its fury : shut up
in himself, no outlet to a friend, no alleviation of woe, no
hope in God. Truly, nothing but firm determination
could have maintained him in this chilling loneliness.
The mission to Nineveh would not have required greater
strength for its accomplishment; and how much nobler
would have been the result ! Are we not equally guilty
of this soul-waste ? It is seen in the *totally wicked* ;
lavishing his manhood in frivolities which weaken, in
pursuits which ruin. Whereas the same power, running
in another line, would invest life with decided purpose,
extensive influence, and a moral supremacy worthy of
heaven. Power is also misappropriated by the *occasionally disobedient*. Their heart purpose is true, but its
life expression, and beauty, is dimmed by recurrent
flakes of sin. The most prominent effort of the soul
is towards God; but hostile seductions have lured to
minor objects, calculated to debase their worshipping
instinct. But even these deceptions, if sanctified by
prayer, instead of dashing upon the rocks would guide
safely unto the haven. This misemployment of moral
power is characteristic of society. Our deepest soul
energies are emitted at the secular value of life, while the
truant impulse finds outlet in the religious : or, to
change the figure, we may say, that commercial enterprises ride upon the full tide of effort, while church matters
float upon the ebbing current. If, then, you are
guilty in this respect, think not that the storm will

pass over; it only delays to gather voice for louder rebuke.

The folly of Jonah is further seen in that *he took the difficulties of life into his own hand.* He sailed to Tarshish. The ocean of life is only navigable with God in the vessel, He alone can guide our helm; and anyone voyaging without Him will soon be made to reef his sails. The darkness of the sky, the rush of the wave, the beating of the gale, will unitedly articulate his doom. Is not experience confirmatory of this? A message came to you, enjoining duty which clashed with preconcerted life plans. You resisted, sailed, and were wrecked; escaping from the deep, only to wander in the tangled forest, haunted by ghostly visions. There, amid a stillness indicative of a nobler Presence, you lay wearily upon the ground. At length energy returned, but it was the force of madness and not of prayer. You rose to your feet, struck God from your life; looked at the forest tracks; selected one; and commenced unarmed, the lonely journey of a rebellious spirit.

Again, we find, that Jonah, trying to extricate himself from difficulty, *facilitated his own punishment.* He went on-to the *sea;* and thus rendered himself liable to the fury of its billows. Had he remained on land this could not have been the case. True, God might have found another method of punishment, but perhaps not so adapted to the harmony of natural law. So it generally happens, that at critical times like these, disobedient men prosecute artifices most unlikely to succeed; easily overthrown, and totally incompatible with forethought. Then the Divine Being takes hold of their folly and makes it the medium of retributive grief.

The folly of Jonah is further noticeable in that *he permitted his conduct to belie his creed.* He fled from the presence of the Lord! What are we to understand by this? As a prophet he must have credited the Omnipresence of God. Did he intend to avoid from his special presence as living in Israel? Surely this would have involved useless trouble, because distance could never have removed him from the touch of the Divine hand. The phraseology of this verse is familiar to us. We designate England the home of Justice; and multitudes, infringing her laws, take refuge in flight. Equity, in a smaller degree, exists in the country to which they hasten, yet they flee from the presence of Justice; and the futility of the attempt is often witnessed in their immediate arrest upon the landing stage of the desired port. Flight appears to throw a charm over the guilty spirit, calming its trouble, disarming its fear, and rekindling hope, again to be striken by disappointment.

Here is seen *the weakness of even a good man's creed.* No word in the language is so abused as creed. It does not mean belief, but character. Anything short of this is mere opinion. Estimated by this standard, how many of us are Atheists and Idolaters! Believing in God, yet practically denying Him by indifference; divesting Him of His attributes, and so worshipping a fiction of the mind. What we need is that Christian Pantheism which feels God everywhere. The effect of which would be to transform human character into a reflection of the angelic. Why is it that our creed has such little influence upon us? Has it waned into the incapacity of death, or into the stupor of exhaustion? Is its

langour occasioned by mental indolence ? Does your
creed embody personal thought and effort ? Are you
convinced of its accuracy? If not, moral debility is inevitable. Is spiritual inactivity the cause of weakness ?
Your creed, intelligently examined, has emerged from
the painful experience of doubt to the joy of conviction; but your heart-fires have not kindled the cold
dogma into.the spontanity of enthusiasm ; and nothing
short of this will place in the hands of creed the sceptre
over human life.

   Now consider, *the expense of this disobedience.*
Jonah paid the "fare." Booking clerks little know the
history of those presenting themselves for railway
tickets.   Some,—the children of misfortune, taking
refuge from ungodly threats ; others, driven by poverty,
are lured to foreign climes by the delusive hope of
wealth ; while many by unknown flight urge their way
to the rim of existence, that in solitude they may hide
the dark enigma of their lives. Thus, if the moral
record of one train were penned, what disclosures
would be made ; many leaving a wretched past ; others
entering upon a joyous future. But Divine mercy curtains
the troubled spirit from the intruding gaze of others,
wrapping it in the mystery of self, penetrated only by
God. Thus, even a disobedient prophet may pass unknown amongst the bustling travellers to Tarshish. He
paid the fare. Sin is always expensive. Its habits are extravagant, and frequently money is necessary to deliver
from their penalty. Look at that home, comfortless and
drear; its young mistress, with anxious countenance,
and hectic flush, stands before you, trying to hide her
renegade tears in the caresses of her little one—*that*

is the fare the drunkard pays. The young man of pious
home gets a situation, his commercial prospects widen;
sinful companions gather about his path—they lead him
to the card table—till the fiend that smiled upon his
innocence to endanger, now tramples upon it to
destroy. His debts are required, and to free himself
from their constant terror, he steals; detection
ensues; and *a ruined character is the fare he pays.*
Another young man, finding himself in a large city for
commercial toil rushes at once into its gaiety, his
nights are spent in profligate revels; soon his cheeks
pale, weakness seizes him; and *a broken constitution is
the fare he pays.* And, how many are there in this
very city paying, as by instalments, this awful price?
The cries of the poor, the tears of the sorrowful, the
agonies of the dying, with one hollow voice announce
the fare to Tarshish. Do we address a passenger about
to step on board the vessel, halt my brother, go not
down into her; you cannot afford to pay such a fare,
especially when the same money will take you to
Nineveh. Is the ship well built? is the weather fine?
It may be now; but *wait till you get out to sea,* and
then talk about your prospects.

　　Reflect now on the *criminality* of this resistance.
It was *wilful.* Jonah deliberately paid his money, and
despising all likelihood of danger, closed the bright
history of the past to open the dark tragedy of the
future. It was also *ungrateful.* God had honored
Jonah by entrusting him with the commission; what,
therefore, could be more ungrateful than denial?
The flower may refuse to open its petals to the sunbeam, but how can an immortal soul close itself to the

privilege and dignity of a God-sent message? Then,
Jonah's disobedience was *continuous*. It was a night
without one star. Some men never break the fall of their
moral nature. They go all the way to Tarshish without a
stoppage. While Jonah was paying for his ticket, the
act should have stimulated thought ending in a return
to duty. But no! now he has sailed. But whither?
Who can tell? His passport says Tarshish. But God
has issued another for the waters of the mighty
deep. Sin has not always the power to execute its
contract. Oh! disobedient one we warn you that the
ticket for Tarshish is no guarantee for your arrival
thither. Hasten out of the ship, or your next home
may be in the great deep!

Finally, this verse teaches us that *circumstances are
sometimes favourable to resistance.* "And he found a
ship going to Tarshish." When once the man is determined to flee from God, the means will soon be found.
There are plenty of ships chartered for this purpose, all
waiting at the quay of human life. But this consideration
does not paliate guilt; because, though the vessel is
ready, you are not obliged to enter, and in that you do
so consists your condemnation. *Never measure disobedience by apparent success.* There is a future yet to
come. It is a part of the great method of life that we
should be tested by the inviting presence of wrong;
therefore, do not turn opportunity into providence, but
regard it as the merchantman of evil. The youth of
selfish inclination finds that his master has unknowingly
left the till open; the amount therein is large, a trifle
could not be missed, and he is alone—the ship is found
—he embarks; then comes the storm. He could not cen-

sure the opportunity, but the disposition which prompted
him to embrace it. What then is the direction of your
life? toward Tarshish or Nineveh? If the former,
think of your doom; if the latter, rejoice in your hope.

But the Lord sent out a great wind into the sea, and there was
a mighty tempest in the sea, so that the ship was like to be broken.
Ver. 4.

This verse teaches the moral significance of the
weather. The wind was caused by the disobedience of
Jonah. That the weather has a meaning ulterior to
itself none can question, though so few comprehend it.
We rise from our bed, and, drawing aside the curtain,
announce the morning to be fine. But how rarely do
we look beyond the clear sky, or the moody grandeur
of the East, about to streak the heavens with vermillion
tints. Or, if tempestuous, thought finds its terminus
in the pattering rain, or inclement wind: instead of
hastening to their prompting cause. Why is the morning thus? Is the noble action of an unknown life
casting out its beauty in the sunshine, or is moral
delinquency striking its deep notes in the wild sym-
phonies of the hurricane? True, only God can answer
the question; but that we ask it, is a proof of reverent
feeling, the utterance of which gives relief to the heart.
Is it thought impossible that the multifarious attitudes
of character should find expression in the weather?
But why? Is not the weather equally varied, and why
should it not, therefore, become the exponent of moral
life? No doubt, at times, God views character in a
representative aspect. Its most prominent types stand
in His Presence, and the penalty announced, or the
reward bestowed, includes all minor lives of a kindred

condition. So it may be with the weather. The most holy, being privileged with that adapted to their good; while the wicked are driven before the wind. True, this is beyond explanation, but the mystery instead of filling with incredulity should inspire solemnity. As God holds the winds in His fist, so he directs the unfettered action of our moral life; and by an unknown method accommodates each to the other. Do we not feel that nature bears an unspoken relationship to us? Does it not influence our lower being, producing either a dull melancholy or a glad light-heartedness? The sunbeam touches our nature into music; while black clouds find our harps upon the willows, plaintively awaiting the brightness of another day. And if this connection exists in the trivial matter of happiness, what association will there be found in the deeper affinities of our being, which have reference to goodness. If the weather is linked to the human side of our life, surely it will be to the Divine. And this adaptation of weather to character is equally true of national history. We assert that the crops are plentiful or meagre; that the epidemic rages amongst our herds; that men are being stricken by the plague—what is this but saying in other words that national life, both in its physical bearing and moral destiny is allied to atmospherical influences? Lord Macaulay, writing upon the coming of Prince William to England, says, "The weather had, indeed, served the Protestant cause so well, that some men of more piety than judgment, fully believed the ordinary laws of nature to have been suspended for the preservation of the liberty and religion of England. Exactly a hundred years before, they said, the Armada,

invincible by man, had been scattered by the wrath of
God. Civil freedom and Divine truth were again in
jeopardy; and again the obedient elements had fought
for the good cause. The wind had blown strong from
the east while the Prince wished to sail down the
Channel, had turned to the south when he wished to
enter Torbay, had sunk to a calm during the disembarkation, and, as soon as the disembarkation was
completed, had risen to a storm, and had met the pur-
suers in the face." We think that this brilliant sneer
is totally unwarranted. Is not Protestantism the cause
of God? Is there, therefore, anything superstitious in
believing that He will protect it from eminent peril?
If the combinations of nature are ordered by Him,
what more natural than that they should be made the
servants of His will, and commissioned for the welfare of His church? Again, is not the moral higher
than the physical, and thus may we not reasonably
expect that the latter shall minister to the former?
Prince William was the representative of Protestant
truth, and King James of Roman Catholic intolerance;
the weather aided the interests of the former, and what
more proper than that its ministry should be associated
with Divine power? This beautifully written sneer is but
a flower fastened to a dead body. The passage demonstrates, by the veracity of its facts, that there is a moral
significance in the weather, and lamentably proves that
even the keenest intellects have failed to perceive what the
untutored have devoutly acknowledged. Thus, we find,
that the weather is not arbitrarily assigned by dogmatic
power; that it is not meaningless; that it is not sent
merely to ripen the crops, or to complete the seasons;

but as the embodiment and exponent of moral character. If we could but read the lesson of every storm,
and articulate the moaning of every wind, what revelations would be made of human life ! How many Jonahs
should we discover fleeing from the presence of the
Lord !

Here we learn that *the phenomena of material nature
are occasioned by God.* " The Lord sent out a great wind
into the sea." There is a tendency abroad to regard the
world as a piece of mechanism ; complete in structure,
independent of external control, and final in its operation. This is partly owing to the ambiguity of the Divine
agency. Men do not see the hand of God outstretched ;
lifting the planets into space, and hurling them on their
missions.   And, to unhallowed thought, which only
finds contentment in visible objects, this Divine reserve
is fatal to its supernatural character.   While others,
feeling the absolute necessity of a motive force, beholding the regularity of nature, invest an unknown something, called law, with the attributes of God.   Again,
the voice of infidel science, alleging the incongruity of
scripture, and its antagonism to the theories of advanc-
ing knowledge, has created in the public mind deroga-
tory ideas of God, which have found their ultimate
issue in Atheism.   Also, timid Christians, whose deepest feelings have been those of reverence, thinking it
incredible that God would ally himself to the trivialities
of life, have confirmed society in this attitude of doubt.
Thus, educated by these extremes of thought, many
seem to imagine, either that the world is governed by
the force of an original impulse, or by the inherent
strength of its own law.   But, although the Divine

Being thus conceals himself from view, He nevertheless orders the workings of nature. True, they are regulated by Law, but Law is only a synonyme for God. The distinction which men make between God and natural Law, is more idea than fact. They are one. There cannot be Law without God, neither can there be God without Law; and infidelity consists in their separation. Thus, it is not in the nature of things that God is detached from natural Law, but by our defective perception thereof; and the unhealthy condition of moral feeling induced thereby, is a sufficient demonstration of error. In this oneness of Monarch and Law, human governments present no analogy. Earthly sovereigns are not independent; they do not always originate their laws; they are unduly influenced by circumstances over which they have no control; they have to base their legislation on principles already established. Whereas, the Divine Being is supreme, unmoved by the contingencies of life, untouched by the revolutions of change, and incapable of weakness through unavoidable infirmity: His Laws, intuitive, are the natural outcome of His will, and therefore inseparable from himself. What confidence should this reflection inspire; that the forces of nature are not independent of God, but one with Him in all His movements; and, therefore, can never be stimulated by any frantic impulse to overstep their limit, or disobey His will. Here we find that the storm, both as to the time of its occurrence, and the extent of its fury, was under Divine command. What consolation should this verse administer to the heart of the lonely wife as she hears the rattle of the gale, and thinks of her husband upon the mighty deep.

She can trust in God, knowing that He sits above the storm; consequently that it is not a reckless confusion of the elements, but a means ordained for moral good.

Further, we learn here that *the operations of God are sometimes violent in their nature.* Coverdale renders it, "but the Lord hurled a great wynde into the sea," thus giving greater emphasis, than our version, to the forcefulness of the Divine action. How frequently during the last half-century have our public journals recorded incidents in harmony with the teaching of this verse: from the eruptions of burning mountains; the earthquakes which have submerged islands; and the lightning which has occasioned immediate death, we learn that the Divine Being has powers within His nature, which if brought into exercise, would bury the world in one vault of ruin. But while we are awed by this reflection, let us also be cheered by remembering that God is also characterised by that gentleness which can only whisper its mercy in the breeze.

We find also from this verse *that the guilt of one man often endangers the safety of others.* The Law of vicarious suffering pervades society. Its necessity was exhibited, and its rectitude established, by the death of Christ on the cross; and in proportion as we imbibe the principle of that sacrifice, calmed by its pathos, touched by its love, and fortified by its hope, shall we cheerfully acquiesce in this mysterious arrangement of human life. The misconduct of a prominent statesman may lay waste a nation; the folly of a municipal council may disorder a metropolis; and the prodigality of a son may ruin a family. Men are so intimately associated that they touch each other at the most inconceivable points. As one great law pervades the solar system, holding it in a harmony which would be broken by the divergence of one star from its orbit ; so society is regulated by laws which none can infringe without correlative harm. But while this principle of unity is the occasion of grief, it is also the medium of joy, as the same inexplicable combination of life, is alike the portal of happiness and woe. But although this method of Providence is surrounded by much ambiguity, sufficient light is given to prevent error. We must never shrink from admitting the Sovereignty of Divine Providence, else an irreverent disposition will prevent a true appreciation of its design. The rectitude of God, and the safety of man, alike consist in the inherent supremacy of the Divine will. Nor should we regard the regality of human Monarchs as typal of the Divine; for while the former may become despotic, the latter cannot; else absolute power would degenerate into incomparable weakness. Thus, Divine Sovereignty is its own voucher, and the justice of its mystery is guaranteed and illuminated by the occasional gleams of light, which shine from less intricate Providences. This verse clearly teaches that the Providence of God is not purposeless, but restorative, to bring back from flight, and punitive to chastise for disobedience. As regards the mariners, the storm was of a developing tendency, bringing into exercise deep religious feeling. Thus its moral benefit to the sailors exhibits the mercy of God; while the character of their past lives, as idolaters is a sufficient vindication of His justice. But, although these reflections show the equity of God's dealings with us in the associations of life; that He does not make them a medium of arbitrary pain; they do not extricate Jonah from the guilt of endangering the safety of others. Now he becomes chargeable with a twofold sin; of disobedience against God, and of injury, which might have terminated in death, to his fellows. Jonah became the point of contact between the retributive vengeance of God, and the sin of these unholy men. There are multitudes who stand in this relation to their fellow creatures. Nor is the church clear of such persons; many by their hypocrisy bring disgrace upon themselves, suspicion upon others, and introduce elements of woe into this the most solemn of all communities. We must be careful in this respect, lest our conduct should kindle fires which may burn the stubble of other lives.

This passage might be regarded *in a typical light*: the ship as representative of human life; the wind as illustrative of all adverse influences; and the quelling of the storm when the vessel was like to be broken, as exhibiting the restraining power of God in His dealing with human nature. But as the direct teaching of the verse is so instructive, we have preferred listening to its voice; regarding the typal as of minor importance.

> Then the mariners were afraid, and cried every man unto his god, and cast forth the wares that were in the ship into the sea, to lighten it of them. But Jonah was gone down into the sides of the ship; and he lay, and was fast asleep.—*Ver.* 5.

This verse teaches *the moral effects of a storm.* It filled with *timidity.* "The mariners were afraid." Nor was their terror uncalled for. How furious must have been the gale thus to have disquieted them. It was no phantom rising from the deep, that struck terror to their hearts; but a most unaccountable reality, whose awfulness they individually felt. There are missions to be fulfilled, at the critical junctures of personal history, of such vast importance, that God calls His most authoritative messengers; and these appearing to the view of man, encircled by the light of another world, fill him with apprehension. The storm also inspired with *reverence*. There are times in life when man must be solemn. We are placed in circumstances so unmistakably the result of Divine intervention; so forceful in their bearing upon the soul, that conscious of a noble, and holy Presence, the oath of blasphemy is hushed in the prayer for help.

Such was the case with these sailors. And when we remember that they were heathens, do we not gather from their conduct, *how firmly rooted in the human heart is the idea of a God?* Each mariner had a deity to whom he appealed in this extremity of peril. Belief in a God is almost universal. Only one race of people has been found totally destitute of religious feeling, and, consequently, ignorant of a Supernatural being. If the supposition, that the Adamanese have no Divinity, is correct,* the fact proves that our knowledge of God is the result of Revelation, and not of

---

*Having retained his native language, he gave them an account of his adventure; and, as the Adamanese have no notions of a deity, he acquainted them with the knowledge he had of God, and would have persuaded his countrymen to learn of him the way to adore God and to obey His laws; but he could make no converts. — *Hamilton's Account of the East Indies in Pinkerton's Voyages.*

intuition. That the exception is a solitary one shows how tenaciously the human soul clings to the idea of God; making it the font of its joy, and the inspiration of its life. Manhood without God is drear and helpless; and trembling in this frigid latitude, its hand is outstretched for something to kindle its feeling and excite its hope. But, although men almost instinctively believe in the existence of a Supernatural Being in circumstances of danger the conviction is more intensely realized, and becomes a stimulus to prayer. Difficulty is the great refutation of Atheism. The man who has written the most sceptical books, who has advanced the most un-scrupulous arguments, who has derided the honest confidence of the pious, when in perplexity, refutes all his logic by the pallor of his countenance, and the tremor of his lips, as they mutter an inarticulate plea for help. The weakness of man, at such times of grief, becomes an argument for exterior aid; its source may be unknown, its nature undefined; but existing some-where, endowed with the power to help. And what is this but God? True, such a belief is indefinite, but if retained it will be touched into distinctness by the life-giving energy of the Holy Spirit.

This verse demonstrates *the inability of natural Revelation* to unfold the important doctrines so inti-mately allied to the welfare of our moral life. These sailors were idolaters. They cried every man unto his god. Material nature does not, universally, teach the unity of the Divine Being. Perhaps the deep underlying harmony of nature, the essential prevalence of its law, and the unchanging operation of its forces, might instruct the contemplative student: but to the unthink-

ing, by far in the majority, there is such an apparent
diversity of colour and shape, there are such rapid
transitions from calm to storm, that they are immediately
attributed to the movements of contending Deities.
Hence, while to one mind, nature teaches the oneness
of God; to another, it may inculcate Polytheism; and
in that it leaves error possible, through defective instruction, on so vital a subject, consists its weakness.
Thus man, in the absence of inspired truth, is left in
uncertainty respecting the Divine character; then the
mind, striving to realize the unknown God, unduly
influenced by imagination, is brought to worship the
creation of its own fancy. And so the character of
Deity is made to depend upon the mental and moral
idiosyncrasy of the worshipper. And each man calls
upon *his* god. If Polytheism were true, what confusion
would it occasion in the world. Lives, opposed to
each other, supported by antagonistic powers, would be
in constant feud; while even those in apparent harmony
would be exposed to the peril of fitful change.

Next we find that *these mariners betake themselves
to prayer.* Men who never pray in prosperous circumstances, are generally the first to call upon God, when
surrounded by difficulty. Thus, we might enquire
whether these prayers were a selfish outcry for help,
or the embodiment of penitent feeling? Were they
heard? Did some unspoken attitude of soul, or did
their fervor, render them acceptable to God? We
cannot tell, but will charitably hope they met with a
helpful response. These prayers were *earnest.* "They
cried every man unto his god." The fierceness of the
tempest, and their felt nearness to some uncontrollable

Power, no doubt contributed to this urgency of petition. Might we not as a Christian church profitably imitate, in this respect, the example of these sailors? Are not our supplications too cold and formal, almost devoid of life? Can we expect that such weak effort will touch the heart of God? Whereas, if our devotion was characterised by deeper earnestness, would it not result in greater benefit? Again, their prayers were *unanimous*. "They cried *every man* unto his god." Amongst that heathen crew there was not one knee unbent; every hand was outstretched in pleading attitude. So terrible was the storm that all effort appeared useless; and the Captain, instead of trying to shout his commands above the raging elements, cried to his god; and his comrades, instead of running about the vessel, and climbing its rigging, joined in his entreaties for calm. Never do we feel our weakness more than when in contact with physical danger. Totally impotent, our only refuge is in prayer to God. May we not, as a church, also learn something from the combined effort of these mariners? Without mutiny amongst themselves, one in sympathy and desire, together they faced a common danger. Should we not, as a Christian people, be thus united, that when assailed by difficulty, instead of being debilitated by factions, we may be fortified by union. Oneness of thought and feeling is the strength and condition of collective supplication. The solo of prayer; the petition of one holy life is beautiful and potent, but in the Handel chorus of prayer, consists our church-strength. This storm also called forth *prudence*. "They cast forth the wares that were in the ship into the sea, to lighten it of them." This shows how tena-

ciously men cling to life. How, that when in circumstances of extremity, thought fixes itself upon personal
safety, regarding all other matters as of minor import.
Then, treasures of the greatest value, which have cost
years of anxious toil, and perhaps health itself, to
accumulate, are sacrificed without regret. Thus, how
uncertain are the things which constitute the secondary
enjoyment of our lives! how foolish to unduly estimate
and make them our primary hope, when any moment,
circumstances may arise, which, putting them beyond
our reach, shall rob the present of its joy, and the
future of its solace!

This verse also exhibits *the contrasts noticeable in the
same circle of life.* For, while the sailors are all praying, Jonah, in the very same vessel, is asleep. Why is
he asleep? Probably, his nature, exhausted by the
fatigue and grief of the last few days, now finds relief
in slumber. In this cradle of the mighty deep he is
rocked, by the tempest, into a total unconsciousness of
danger. Does not this scene find its counterpart in
the *church?* Many are praying for reviving influences,
impressed by an alarming sense of want, they rise to
great fervor of soul, but while these are thus employed,
there are others careless and indifferent—almost, if not
quite, asleep. So in the *domestic circle,* nearly the
whole family is converted, holy influences pervade the
home; but there is one son unsaved—alone in this condition, presenting a deep contrast to the rest, he sleeps
in the sides of the vessel. Are our lives thus a contrast; our voices being silent while others are praying?

So the shipmaster came to him, and said unto him, What meanest thou, O sleeper? arise, call upon thy God, if so be that God will think upon us, that we perish not.—*Verse* 6.

This verse shows *how far disobedience leads from the proper missions of life.* Instead of being at Nineveh Jonah is fast asleep. When once we are determined to resist Providence, and the first step has been taken, no one can predict the ultimate issue. In all probability we shall go from one sin to another; and, in proportion to the greatness and purity of our Prophet-life, will be the deepness of our fall. Have we not many times painfully felt, how far one act of disobedience has removed us from the destined path of rectitude. And how *weakening* is the moral condition induced by this divergence from duty. The soul, instead of being occupied with invigorating work; instead of being disciplined by contact with the greater difficulties of Nineveh, is enervated by an unnatural sleep. And thus a manhood, capable of the highest effort, degenerates into a senseless inactivity.

God employs instrumentalities to reclaim the disobedient from their sin. "So the *shipmaster* came to him." Great natures are not to be wholly given up without strong endeavours for their recovery. Hence, God not only sent the tempest to bring back Jonah, but also the shipmaster to convince him of his folly. We have many times been guilty of flight from God; of degrading our manhood by association with idolaters; but, when in the darkest passage of our sin, a messenger came urging us to repent. And, to-day, as we review the past, do we not recognise in that over-

whelming trouble, in that commercial failure, in that
family bereavement, the burly shipmaster who cried to
our guilty souls, " What meanest thou ? " These instrumentalities are frequently *harsh*. Would not the
voice of this Captain appeal sternly in the ears of
Jonah ? The shipmaster was astonished at the spectacle before him ; there appeared something about it
that he could not understand, consequently, he addressed the sleeper in language calculated to obtain an
explanation. Not that he was animated by caprice or
malice, but by the best of motives, no doubt thinking
it wise, both for the safety of Jonah, and for the satis-
faction of the crew, to awaken, and ascertain the meaning of the sleeper's apparent indifference, to their circumstances of peril. So it sometimes happens that when good
people backslide, their conduct astonishes, and becomes
quite inexplicable to onlookers, who not having marked
any open profanity, are ignorant of their heart apostacy.
And perhaps giving utterance to this feeling of surprise in the question, " What meanest thou ? They,
unknowingly, become an instrument, in the Divine
hand, of conviction to a disobedient Prophet. These
instrumentalities are also *humiliating*. Was it not
so for a Prophet of the Lord to be rebuked by a
heathen Pilot ? Surely, the shipmaster is the Prophet
now, rebuking the disobedient, and urging the careless
to thoughtfulness. How frequently are even churches,
and their members, reproved by the inquiries of unthinking men ? Their conduct is so undignified, their
effort so indifferent, and their sins are so apparent, that
they either lay themselves open to the reproach of the
scoffer, or to the pitiful lament of the holy. When

will the church by her consistency, by the beauty of
her morality, the purity of her life, and the harmony
of her members, render such reproach not only unnecessary, but impossible? These instrumentalities
are *faithful* in their dealing with us. The shipmaster
did not flatter Jonah, but addressed him in his true
character of sleeper. So the means which God employs to convert us, often expose the weakness of our
character, and the sin of our life. But, however rough
these measures may appear, do not repine; but rejoice
in that they are angels designed to lead you back to
God. Listen to their pleading voice, and heed their
message.

Finally, this verse shows, *a heathen's belief in the
doctrine of prayer*. " Arise, call upon thy God, if so
be that God will think upon us, that we perish not."
Thus this heathen shipmaster not only recognized the
necessity of prayer, but also the duty of pleading for
others. Did he think that there was something remarkable, some unknown greatness connected with the
strange demeanour of the sleeper before him, and that,
therefore, his supplications would have greater influence
with the gods? Or, did he merely urge Jonah to join
the crew in their prayer for help, without any supposition of his superiority to them? We cannot say. Deep
rooted in the human soul is the need of intercessory
prayer. Men feel, if they cannot tell why, if they do
not know how, that they must pray for each other.
And such feelings, awakened in the captain by the
raging of the storm, thus found utterance.

He also believed *in prayer as influencing God and
moving Him to the protection of human life*. " If so be

that God will think upon us that we perish not." Many writers allege that God is unmoved by prayer, and that our petitions simply influence the worshipper, by inducing in his heart feelings of contrition and resignation, which bring him into harmony with the irrevocable decree of the Divine will; and thus prayer, instead of meeting with a true response, and being the means of definite blessing, becomes little more than a pitiful cry for help, which, though heard, must virtually remain unaided. We would not assert, in fact it would be foolish to do so, that the creed of this heathen pilot was more orthodox; or, that his insight into the doctrine of prayer was clearer than many holding the theory above mentioned; but the storm having swept away all pre-concerted notions, and all unholy prejudice, and having no time for speculative thought, he was left to the guidance of impulse, which is frequently more to be trusted, in matters of deep importance than logic, and thus, going beyond his own narrow theology, he uttered in this brief sentence the true doctrine of supplication. This error, respecting prayer, may be attributable to the fact that many thinkers have given unlawful prominence to the Divine Unchangeableness. But this mistake, cannot but lead to wrong conclusions; as the character of God is equally balanced in all its parts, and therefore His Benevolence must be equal to His Immutability; and as prayer cannot alter the latter, neither can it invalidate the former. Is not the Immutability of God exhibited in that unchanging love, which, smiling upon the contrite heart, answers its petition, as will most enhance its moral good? If we pray for anything not in harmony with the interests of our higher nature, God will not bestow it, as His Infinite Benevolence could never consent to our spiritual injury. That God is influenced by true supplication is abundantly demonstrated, both by sacred history, and human experience ; and that Love is the motive of response few can deny.

Here we also learn *how totally ignorant men are of our inner life*. Jonah is urged to prayer, which fact clearly proves that his disobedience was unknown to the heathen pilot, or he would not have called him to a duty for which he was so unfit, but would rather have issued an order of immediate arrest. People look upon our exterior demeanour, and taking it as an index to our thought and feeling, are frequently deceived. This Captain, no doubt, thought that Jonah was far better off than any of the crew; they, in deep agony of soul, were crying to their Deities; while he, ignorant of the tempest, was rocked by its fury into deeper slumber. They appear to be in the very arms of terror, while he enjoys the tranquility of repose. But how delusive this outward appearance ! Light is caused by the terrific lightning as well as by the gentle sunbeam. So there is a sleep occasioned by the wild grief of despair as also by the light fatigue of honest labour. Were the mariners troubled by the storm, and was not Jonah harrassed by his flight from God ? If they feared those darkened clouds, those ruthless waves, that reeling ship; Jonah likewise trembled before an offended God, of whose retributive anger this tempest was but a faint image. Thus, although the Captain urges him to pray, he cannot with this heavy sin pressing upon his nature, while hope appears excluded from the future. No! the disobedient Prophet is neither in the proper frame of mind, nor is he in the fit place for prayer. Jonah must become penitent in heart, he must get out of the ship, away from his crimes, and return to God, before he can bow in hopeful devotion. The narrative does not inform us that the Prophet did respond to the wish of the Captain, although he may have done so. As he awoke, and heard the storm beating about him, and saw the waves leaping from their depths, some uncontrollable, unknown, impulse may have brought him to his knees : the noble habit of his former life, prevailing over disobedience, may have uttered its plea for pardon ; or to avoid further suspicion, he may have followed the example of the mariners. But the narrative, although silent on the matter, would almost indicate that such was not the case ; but that the question which awoke the Prophet from sleep, also aroused his soul to reflection ; and, being deeply moved by surrounding circumstances, it would appear that he was speechless for a time, until conviction being intensified by the casting of the lot, he yielded himself to nobler feeling, and confessed the dark history of his guilt. There are times when men sink to their lowest level of moral character ; and then comes the crisis, either ruinous or hopeful ; and frequently at this point, the apostate life is touched into new beauty, by the still power of another world ; as midnight is soon tinted by the light of morning dawn. Hence the disobedient Prophet rises from his degradation, though most painful experiences yet await, to discipline, and fit him for the destined mission to Nineveh. If these words should reach one, whose character once fair, is now dark with impurity ; having fled from God, the faculties of your Being have deteriorated in moral worth, and you stand a broken wreck in the presence of awakening influences. Be thankful for them, yield to their touch, that you may yet be restored to perfection of life, and to office in the church.

And they said every one to his fellow, Come, and let us cast lots, that we may know for whose cause this evil is upon us. So they cast lots, and the lot fell upon Jonah.—*Verse 7.*

In this verse we see *human nature in a dreadful extremity*. Hearing Jonah accosted in the language of the previous verse, the mariners have gathered about him, probably hoping that he may discover to them the meaning of this increasing tempest. Prayer having apparently failed, they now think it time to employ another precaution; hence trial by lot being suggested, the culprit is immediately detected. When in trouble human nature becomes very *ingenious*. The perplexed, having vainly tried one method of relief, successively venture upon other expedients, until the remedy is attained. Perhaps, the dullest man, when in grief through domestic bereavement, or commercial failure, becomes the most inventive genius ; then he contrives with such perspicuity, that his compeers are amazed at his fortune. Hence, difficulty exhibits our real worth, manifesting originality, developing latent power, and begetting within us thought, which, being transmuted into determined effort, lifts the hitherto stagnant life high above its ordinary level. Also when in trouble, human nature becomes most *sympathetic*. "And they said every one to his fellow." There was no independent member, no mutinous spirit amongst the crew; no one suggested another way of relief; all, as though animated by one common impulse, at once accept this test of innocence. Great sorrow has a uniting tendency. Men, who have been the most inveterate enemies, seldom found in commercial relationship, and never in private intercourse, by an unforseen circumstance, have been brought together, and overtaken by a general calamity, their enmity has ceased, animosity has been forgotten, and, looking upon their united consultation, and effort, you might have imagined them to be the closest friends.

Further, this verse shows that even heathen mariners recognized the fact *that human suffering is occasioned by misdoing.* "That we may know for whose cause this evil is upon us." They did not attribute their grief, to the arbitrary allotment of tyrannic power, to the mishap of uncontrollable forces, or to the indifference of God, but to an unknown cause existing amongst themselves. And here these mariners teach a mournful fact which should beget within us diligent self-examination of motive, and life; fervent contrition of heart, and deep humility of spirit. In the garden of Eden grief was unknown, amid the purity of heaven its sigh is unheard; but the road of this probationary life is strewn with flowers, whose beauty is marred, whose fragrance is poisoned, and whose stems are covered with thorns. True, human suffering, as to its primary origin, and ultimate issue, is a dark problem; but as concerning us, the most important truth is, that evil is its cause. Whether we enquire into the devasta-

tion of life by the pestilence; the blight of our crops
by the continuance of unsuitable weather; the dire
confusion of the city by the tidings of commercial
panic; the bitter anguish of the parent as he consigns
his loved one to the grave; or into the decreptitude of
the aged, as their energy declines into yet greater
feebleness—the only voice which meets our tears, is
that which proclaims our sin. There is an investigation into this deep mystery which is impious and wrong;
but there is also an induction which is profitable and
just; this latter we commend to you, that, learning the
meaning of grief, you may also find the evil by which
it is occasioned. Therefore, instead of regarding pain
as a demon from Hell come to tear our hearts, and
hush the glad music of our lives; let us look upon it
as a bright angel of the cross, designed to teach the
depravity of our nature, the magnitude of sin, and the
corrective love of God.

This verse also proves *that the Divine Being has
abundant means at His disposal for the discovery of our
sin*. These mariners were entirely ignorant of Jonah's
disobedience, but by the apparently fortuitous casting
of the lot, its whole history was made known. So,
crime may be committed; darkness may hide its enormity; secrecy may render detection difficult; loneliness
may prevent convincing evidence; dexterity may baffle
the cleverest pursuit; but at the point where human
arrangements fail, the Divine Being interposes; and
darkness is illuminated; secresy is intruded upon;
loneliness is terminated; dexterity is turned into folly;
and the entire deed held up to the public view, entails
the stigma, and receives the just condemnation of its

guilt. No one can read the page of national history, or study the retribution of human life, without feeling that God does, in the most inexplicable manner, unfold our hidden faults, causing them to rebound upon the offender with awful effect. True, the disclosure may not be immediate; years may pass in their rapid flight, yea even death may have laid you in the silence of an everlasting future; yet neither the sweep of time, nor the oblivion of the grave, can prevent the discovery of your crime. True, you may be beyond the reach of its legal penalty, but surviving relatives will live to behold the after-light of your posthumous character, dimmed by exposure; and this lapse of time, shall but enhance your guilt, proclaiming the hardihood of a nature, that could carry the dark secret of woe so long, in the unentered chamber of its being. Sometimes, the Divine Being presses the crime so heavily upon the guilty one, that confession is the only outlet of relief; or unconsciously, amidst the quiet of midnight, the mind, whose untiring energies have not yielded to repose, unfolds the deed, declaring unmistakably, the motive which prompted, the circumstances which surrounded, and the results which have followed its committal. Oh! that the omniscience of God, and His certain exposure of evil, may deter us from acting the part of a disobedient Prophet.

Also this verse exhibits *the Divine superintendence of little events*. "The lot fell upon Jonah." Perhaps you may be inclined to designate this casting of the lot a foolish, if not a wicked, appeal to Providence for help. We have many instances in Scripture* where a

---

*Leviticus 16; Numbers 33; Joshua 7; 1 Samuel 10; Acts 1.

like course of conduct has been pursued without censure, and even under the direction of holy men. And we can easily imagine that circumstances might arise in our day, which would justify the same method of procedure. But it ought to be the exception, and should even then be conducted with great solemnity. We must carefully distinguish between such a use of the lot, as a devout appeal to God, when in insolvable difficulty, and its abuse for gambling purposes; the former by earnest prayer, is made a deeply religious act, while the latter is profane, being an atheistic appeal to fate, not only illegal, but immoral. When the lot is used for the election of persons, equally worthy, to occupy honourable positions; or for the choice of men, equally ready, to brave the perils of imminent danger —its use, justified by emergency, is harmless, and those using it may reasonably anticipate the Divine sanction. In this conviction of Jonah, by the mere casting of the die, which was a very trivial event, we have evidence that God presides over the minor details of every day life. Perhaps, a few may consider this detection fortuitous, occasioned more by chance than God, but the Christian man attributes it wholly to the latter; and this conclusion invests the narrative with a moral beauty and a harmony of purpose, which otherwise it would not have; for as the tempest was occasioned by God for the recovery of Jonah, so was the casting of the lot, and both may be equally attributed to Divine intervention. Frequently does God control the minor events of life, causing them to work the purposes of His will; and His Wisdom is seen, in that He can thus adapt them to the exigencies of human behaviour. All the transactions of life, however minute, and all the results of our conduct, however accidental, are under the control of heaven. While this fact should keep the wrong doer in awe, it should also inspire the Godly man with comfort, in that no catastrophe, however great, no incident however trivial, can drop from the great helmet* of human life, without the Divine permission.

Lastly, we are taught by this verse, *that sin frequently brings men into a most unenviable prominence.* Had Jonah been on board the vessel as a pleasure seeking traveller, or engaged about commercial duty, he would probably have reached his destination almost unknown, certainly unquestioned; but now every eye is upon him, and he is the sole topic of conversation. So there are multitudes, who would never have been known beyond the immediate circle of their relatives, had it not been for their deeds of pelf, and murder; myriads have sounded their names into the world's ear, arrested the attention of the busy, and excited the wonder of the curious, merely by the awful daring of their sin. Popularity of this kind is very easily attained; for when the crime is done, there are always trumpeters to blazon it abroad; in these days of public journals, and petty gossip, tidings of evil soon gain publicity; and then their hero becomes the theme of the world's thought and talk. From such notoriety may we be delivered!

---

*"Thus they: then aged Nestor shook the helm
And forth, according to their wash, was thrown
The lot of Ajax;"   *   *   *   *   *

Then said they unto him, Tell us, we pray thee, for whose cause this evil is upon us ? What is thine occupation ? and whence comest thou ? what is thy country ? and of what people art thou ?—*Verse* 8.

The subject of this verse is *the public investigation of a private life.* There are times when such enquiries as the above would be both unnecessary, and impudent. For anyone ordinarily to put such questions, and especially for the crew of a ship, thus to interrogate their passengers, would be the height of presumption. The sanctity of personal life must ever be regarded; but the circumstances in which these mariners are placed, completely justify their examination of Jonah. Sometimes men forfeit the right of unquestioned conduct; and, by their impiety, render necessary the most rigid investigation of their fellows. Thus if two men agree to unite for a commercial purpose; for a time all appears hopeful; but soon through the fraudulent speculation, and cunning concealment of the one, bankruptcy is entailed; then, has not the injured partner a right to demand a full enquiry into the private life, and circumstances, of his defrauder, in order to ascertain the extent of his robbery; how much is irretrievably lost; what may be recovered; and to see if any redress can be obtained ? The rogue has lost all title to privacy, and has rendered himself liable to the most penetrating enquiries. Such was the case with Jonah. He had voluntarily placed himself in a certain relationship to this crew, and as the result they were involved in imminent peril, and therefore it was but natural, that when he was discovered to be the cause, they should pry into his antecedents, striving, if possible, to understand the danger surrounding them.

This investigation was *earnestly pursued*. " Tell us, we pray thee, for whose cause this evil is upon us ? " They were no doubt surprised that the lot should have fallen upon Jonah; his outward appearance was the most unspicious; his dress the most respectable; and his manners the most refined; they therefore became most anxious to know if the detection was really correct. " Tell us," are we right in regarding *you* as the occasion of this tempest ? Time is now of importance to these wearied, frightened, storm-beaten mariners, hence they gather about the Prophet, and urge question after question, likely to elicit the full history of his conduct, and its relation to their peril. So if ever we desire to detect wrong-doing, our search must be diligent, and pointed; an indifferent carelessness, and a lazy inactivity, will make our effort vain; while an imagined charity, which waits for the crime to unfold itself, is but a mockery of right.

This investigation also *exhibited forbearance*. When the lot had discovered the guilty Prophet, the mariners did not vent their passion in shouts of anger, or oaths of blasphemy; nor did they take revenge upon the helpless man before them, by immediately casting him into the seething waters; but controlling all feeling of resentment, they forbearingly enquire of him the story of his life. Does not a lesson of great beauty gleam from the conduct of these men ? teaching us to exhibit a patient kindness towards those who may have injured us, by damaging our trade, maligning our reputation, or blighting our hope, but who may be now within our power, tremblingly awaiting the dictate of imagined revenge; that we ought not, without enquiry, and thought, to consign them to the penalty of their deed, but see if there is anything to explain, or extenuate it; that instead of cutting the tree to the ground, you may graft upon its corrupt branches, the principle of a reformed life.

This investigation was *minute*. "What is thine occupation?" Is it lawful; can it be performed without harm to thy fellow creatures; has it the approval of the gods; art thou a diviner, and is it by the aid of magic that thou hast brought this storm upon us; or hast thou no trade, being merely a vagrant wanderer? "When comest thou?" What is thy nationality; from what place did you come on ship-board; and why art thou thus journeying with us;—art thou a murderer fleeing from the scene of thy villany; a thief escaping from the penalty of fraud, or art thou an outlaw bound for a distant country? And thus the questions came upon Jonah from all present, two or three speaking at once, in their eagerness to know his life history. Who can imagine his painful anxiety, as he utters through the storm, the dark confession of his guilt, and thinks of its probable issue? Might we not profitably search into the moral legality of our calling, and its bearing upon the lives of others; also into the meaning of our present conduct, and its probable destiny. For there is a great truth underlying the investigation of this crew. Their unwhispered feeling was that Jonah's occupation and conduct were connected with their peril. So it is awfully possible that our profession, though honourable in the estimation of mankind; that our trade, though productive of gain, may be such that it cannot be pursued without injury to

others; and thus our wealth becomes the price of social
misery, moral impurity, and national degradation. If
such is the case with us, remember that money can
never compensate for moral loss ; and act accordingly.

And he said unto them, I *am* an Hebrew; and I fear the Lord,
the God of heaven, which hath made the sea and the dry *land.*—
Verse 9.

You have frequently visited that old Abbey now
lying in decay; a few broken walls supported by huge
buttresses, a long cloister, a tesselated altar, and a
number of antiquated tombs, are all that remain to
intimate the extent of its former magnificence. But
as you walk about the ruins, trying to decipher that
inscription upon the grave; or admiring yonder ivy
clinging to the delapidated window; thoughts of other
years come into the soul; and beholding the grey stone,
brightened by the clear light of the sun, you involuntarily exclaim, "How beautiful." Yes ! the very ruins
of the old Abbey are grand, and show themselves to
be the relics of former splendour. So it is with Jonah,
he has almost reached the lowest depth of character ;
he is, morally speaking, a wreck, and yet as the first
light of heaven beams upon his nature, and touches its
nobler feeling into exercise, we behold, even in this
condition of sin, the greatness of his Prophet life; and
while listening to him, we cannot but admire, and
wonder how so great a manhood, could have yielded to
so cowardly a sin.

In this verse we have *an apostate Prophet making a
full acknowledgment of his guilt.* " I am an Hebrew;

and I fear the Lord." The confession was *honest*.
Jonah did not endeavour to hide the fact of his sin;
or to conceal its guilt by palliation or omission, but
frankly acknowledged his flight from duty. No doubt
he would experience a deep conflict within him, prior
to the utterance of this verse; pride would revolt at
making such a disclosure to heathen mariners; cowardice would tremble at their expected reproach; but the
Divine voice within, not altogether hushed, urged the
Prophet to unfold his tale of sin; thus, without a
thought of self, with true humility of soul, he threw
himself upon the mercy of the crew.

Hence we find that *this confession was marked by a
penitent spirit*. This verse is not the language of
bravado; nor is it the apology of a terror stricken
coward; but of one, who, feeling that he has done wrong,
wishes to make all the restoration within his power. Thus
Jonah does not place so much emphasis upon the mere
fact of his flight, as upon its criminality; the mariners
urged him to acknowledge the deed, but he informed
them it was committed against " the God of heaven,
which made the sea and the dry land." Does not all
crime appear presumptuous, when we consider against
whom it is perpetrated? We may go into the street
and bare our breast to the forked lightning, but to sin
against a Being of creative power, who could crush us
with a blow, is indeed folly which a moment's calm
reflection would prevent.

The penitence of Jonah is further seen in that *he
acknowledged the aggravated character of his guilt*. He
declared himself to be a Hebrew, participating in the
advantages of that privileged race; nor was he merely

a private member of that community, but he held one
of its highest offices, being a Prophet of the Lord.
Jonah had been placed in the most favourable circumstances; as the flower receives the sunshine and dew,
so that it may expand its petals, display its beauty, and
emit its fragrance; so the character of this Prophet,
thus planted in such congenial soil, nourished by the
richest benediction of heaven, should have developed
into purity and power, but instead of this we find it in
decay. A Christian man cannot sin like wicked people;
his godly training, his prayers to heaven, his study of
Divine truth, and his attendance upon the means of
Grace, prior to his fall, all tend to aggravate its guilt.

This confession shows *how far a man's life may
degenerate, until it becomes a complete mockery of his
religious profession.* In this vessel, the companion of
a heathen crew, fleeing from God, and yet he says, "I
fear the Lord." The life of Jonah had once, yea only
a few days before, been pure and holy; as the expression of heavenly principle, and the herald of the future,
it was the light of his people, presenting a lonely
counterpart to their ignorance of truth, and neglect of
God. But now the contrast is at an end, and the
moral superiority of the Prophet is brought to a level
with the general apostacy of Israel. How frequently
have we to look back from deeds of impiety, and days
of bitter grief, to the former piety of our lives; then
solitude was occupied with prayer, and our public effort
was for the good of others. But now how changed
our condition, the past has gone, leaving only a remembrance of joy; and contemplating our moral degradation, it appears as though we have been living under the

spell of a dire enchantment. Then, what a contradiction is there between our Christian profession, and our conduct! Many of us make great pretences, but how little do they mean, how trivial is their worth. We profess to keep holy the Sabbath day, and yet how often do we spend it in idleness; to be moral philanthropists, and yet how little we do or give for the benefit of others; many verbally acknowledge a high state of Christian perfection, and yet exhibit unholy tempers, and utter unguarded words. Men ought to know that our lives are Christain without being told. Many people make their church membership the cloak of sin, and when suspicion falls upon them, or detection threatens, they cantingly say, "I fear the Lord," hoping thus to prevent further enquiry. Such was not the case with Jonah; the general habit of his life was holy, and this present condition of sin the exception, hence his regret was not that of the detected hypocrite, but the sorrow of a penitent believer, and exhibits the dark back-ground of even a Prophet's life.

Finally, Jonah in this verse *contrasts the omnipotence of Jehovah with the weakness of the heathen deities worshipped by these mariners*. "And I fear the God of heaven, which made the sea and the dry land." The mariners had been praying, long and fervently, that the sea might be made calm unto them, but in vain; for the heathen divinities were alike unable either to hear or answer such a petition. But the God of Jonah was not thus incompetent to aid an imperiled crew, He could hear their cry, and send immediate relief; for being the creator of the sea, he could also keep it in check. And thus the Prophet, taking advantage of this impressive opportunity, unfolds to the crew the true character of God; perhaps hoping, by spiritual teaching, to compensate for the danger into which he had brought them, Like this crew, many of us have only learnt the true nature of God in times of affliction; not until driven by the tempest, have we found Him to be the refuge of human life; and during such periods of grief, we have enjoyed diviner revelations of heaven, and have been permitted a clearer insight into truth than ever before experienced. Thus Jonah declares the infinite superiority of the true God. The storm was occasioned by the exercise of His power; and the weakness of their opposing deities would be implied in that they could not calm it. So far from being creators, the deities whom they adored, were themselves either imaginary, or the work of men's hands, and therefore inferior to that great Being, whose might they had lately been called to witness.

Then were the men exceedingly afraid, and said unto him, Why hast thou done this? For the men knew that he fled from the presence of the Lord, because he had told them.—*Verse* 10.

This verse shows *how deeply unholy men are affected by a revelation of, and felt contact with, the Supernatural.* Upon the commencement of the tempest we read, " Then the mariners were afraid," verse 5, but now they are described as being " exceedingly afraid." We may, therefore, naturally enquire into the cause of their augmented terror. No doubt the true reply is to be found in the fact that the detection of Jonah's flight, has introduced a *moral element* into the storm, which has filled the crew with fear, by giving them an outlook toward an hitherto unknown God.   At first the sailors only beheld the crested billows, and merely felt the sweeping wind, which they had frequently experienced before in safety, they therefore hoped that the calm of hurricanes gone by would yet come upon them.   But now the storm grows fiercer, until it exceeds anything as yet known to the oldest veteran on board.   All feel an instinctive dread of peril, and beholding the dark clouds, occasionally streaked with flame, their lower natures rise into dismay. Numerous are the instrumentalities which inspire terror; but those connected with crime, and the divine punishment thereof, are the most potent to move the human heart.   An inexplicable something, having the appearance of a human hand, may write in characters of fire unknown words upon the wall of your dwelling, hushing the noise of midnight revelry—Belshazzars face may then grow pale* as he trys to decipher the completed writing; but let the young Daniel come, and proclaim that the " Mene Mene, Tekel Upharsin," articulate the just penalty of the monarch's blasphemy, and then that intensified fear, which is but the prelude of death, will come upon him.† Or supposing that proceeding on a journey you were called to witness natural phenomena, the continuation and severity of which exceeded anything of the kind in your remembrance; you would probably be terror stricken. But if an unknown messenger, coming to your side, should announce the event to be the penalty of sin — how would the communication heighten your fear?   And why?   Simply because you would feel, not merely in contact with material pheno-

---

*Daniel 5:9   †Daniel 5:30

mena, but with God, whose voice now claims attention.
And if such would be the case with us, having a prior
knowledge of God, how much more with these heathen,
who now for the first time hear about Him. Ignorant
of Jehovah, they had hitherto paid the homage of their
lives to dumb idols; who then can imagine their
astonishment upon finding their religion to be a myth?
Oh! what an hour is that when the soul first becomes
conscious that its Deity is a phantom, and its piety a
delusion. None can tell the misery of such a conviction, but those who have experienced its agony. It is
like removing the support from the climbing plant,
which has directed its growth, sheltered its delicacy,
and stimulated its vigour. So when we exhibit to the
heathen the unreality of his imagined Deity, we cut
away the tendrils of his heart from their brightest
hope; the supposed virtue of his past life withers into
decay; and his mind is brought into a state of alternate vacuity and despair. But at such times the Divine
Husbandman does not leave the awakened one to the
caprice of his ignorance, but sending the spring-tide
of holy feeling, lifts the dejected nature into the
peace, and hope of the Gospel. Can we wonder that
these mariners, in this hour of mental conflict, were
exceedingly afraid? For a moment they lived without
a God. He had been taken from them by the revelation of the past few hours; and the Supreme Being,
in all the stern reality of His life, and in the plenitude
of His work, was pictured before their minds. The
idea of God as powerful, is the strongest terror that
can take possession of a sinful heart. Many fulfil, in a
very deep sense, and it may be unknowingly, the

passage of Scripture, "And fear not them which kill
the body, but are not able to kill the soul: but rather
fear him which is able to destroy both soul and body
in hell." * During the last few moments this crew had
gained the experience of a life-time. They had learnt
truths hitherto unknown; and these of the most
important character. And this instruction had not
merely the authority of Jonah, but was also corrobor-
ated by the tempest. Thinking that he had forfeited
all influence with the seamen by his detected flight,
the Prophet made the rough voice of the storm, raging
about them, the voucher of his doctrine, and presented
God as the Creator of the world. This aspect of the
Divine character was likely to inspire terror. Not the
benevolence of God in supplying our every want; not
His mercy in forgiving the penitent sinner, were made
known; but His Omnipotence. And this revelation
being in harmony with the beating of the storm, they
were led to expect immediate death. There is something portentous in the general silence of nature, which
speaks more of judgment than of love; but now her
still small voice had risen into louder tones, which
announced unerringly the supremacy of God.

Then these mariners *regarded God as offended*.
They felt that this Being of power had been grieved
by the conduct of Jonah; and if he, a Prophet of the
Lord, had thus given offence by one act of disobedience,
how would they be regarded, whose entire lives had
been spent in indifference and crime? They felt that
they had fallen into the hands of the Living God, and
that their peril was fully deserved. They knew that

---

*Matthew 10:28

the storm was not a causeless display of rage, else they
would have dared it to the worst, and have shouted
their derision above its fury ; but when men are conscious that their punishment is just, courage is stricken
into feebleness, and the most prominent feeling of the
heart is terror.

Also, these mariners *had nothing to alleviate their
woe.* They could not get rid of the truth which had
lately dawned upon them, and which so much enhanced
their grief. They could have no doubt about the guilt of
Jonah, which had introduced the moral element into
the storm. There could be *no mistake.* " For the men
knew that he fled from the presence of the Lord,
because he had told them." The mariners were not
led by the strange demeanour of the traveller to guess
that he was the culprit; it was not a matter of hear-
say ; there was no room for misgiving ; the facts were
palpable ; the storm was raging ; the dark reality stood
before them, and it was theirs to face it. Thus feeling
their circumstances of peril, they ask Jonah, " Why
hast thou done this ? " This was a *rebuke,* intimating
that Jonah as a Prophet of the Lord ought to have
known better than to have acted thus. Had any member of the crew been guilty of the deed, the sin would
not have been so great, as it might have been mitigated
by ignorance ; whereas in the case of Jonah it is
aggravated by every possible consideration.

It was also an *inquiry.* " Why hast thou done
this ? " You must have had some motive for running
away from God ? have you no excuse to offer for your
conduct ? and do you not now see its folly ? If Jonah
had stayed to put these questions to himself before he

had gone on ship-board, they would have been prevented now; but it is too late, and he must suffer the due penalty of his crime. Are there any here about to commit sin? Reflect, and ask yourself, why? Do you expect that it will result in gain? If so, you are deceived. The storm will come, and then injured companions will ask you, why? Do we address a backslider? If so, we enquire, "Why has thou done this?" Was not the grace of God sufficient to keep you? Was temptation too powerful? Or did you neglect the communion of saints, and so fall gradually into sin? "Why hast thou done this?" You can give no satisfactory reply; "Therefore arise call upon thy God that thou perish not."

Then said they unto him, What shall we do unto thee, that the sea may be calm unto us? for the sea wrought, and was tempestuous. —*Verse* 11.

This verse teaches that *the daily avocations of men are not an infallible index to moral character.* Society has come to regard the sailor of to-day very much in the same light as it viewed the Publican of old, in the time of our Lord. It seems to think that the vessel's cordage defiles the heart as well as the garment; and that toil upon the mighty deep renders men incapable of piety. But, although we gladly admit that this is not necessarily the case, yet can we wonder if it is occasionally true? Very frequently the avocation is taken up as a refuge from the reproach of public opinion; or at the capricious hint of youthful fancy, which has been awakened by the glowing pictures of extravagant fiction. And if undertaken in this spirit, and prompted by this motive, what but the deepest degradation can be anticipated? And this likelihood will be enhanced if we contemplate the subsequent disadvantages of a sea-faring life. The mariner is excluded from those social influences and Christian privileges, which are so requisite to true perfection of manhood. He is almost entirely shut out from the advantages of education; away from the hall of learning, he has to solve his problem without the tuition of superior knowledge. Away from the animating influences of an extended community, his mind, instead of being disciplined by contact with the ever varying modes of national thought, is confined to the conventional opinions of an indifferent few. His work, being to a large extent mechanical in its nature, does not call forth that extension of idea, and that force of effort, which are so helpful to the advancement of our higher life. His associates are few, perhaps taken from the lower order of men; their moral disposition may be unknown or doubtful, and yet with these his life must hold communion; he must hear their talk, imbibe their thoughts; and, such being the case, how can we wonder if the brightness of his moral character should yield to the darkness surrounding it? Then, are not the religious privileges of the mariner few? he is probably unattended by the advice of a Christian minister; unwatched by the solicitations of a devout benevolence; unstrengthened by the rest, and untutored by the teaching of the Sabbath; thus, while he is rocked in the ship, his immortal soul is thrown rudderless upon life's great ocean, to be the sport of its fancy, the bubble of its confusion, and the wreck of its fallacy. Also the sailor's continued exposure to danger, and the necessary familiarity therewith, induce a hardness of disposition which renders him unsusceptable to holy influence, and almost incapable of devotional feeling. But, although it is easy to conceive that the character of our mariners may be defective, yet we are not warranted in placing all under the same condemnation; as those presented to our view in connection with Jonah are evidently men of high moral demeanour. This is abundantly demonstrated by their righteous treatment of the Prophet, if by nothing more. Perhaps their general conduct may not have always reached the standard here exhibited, yet underneath their idolatry there were evident germs of good, perhaps planted by the hand of a devout, but heathen mother, whose unsatisfied heart may have spent its divinest energy in search of the true God. As pearls do not float upon the surface of the ocean, but require the diver to fetch them up; so with the mariner, the true greatness of his nature, and the real beauty of his character may be veiled by much that is rough in manner, and apparently contradictory in life; but, penetrating into his deepest nature, you will find a jewel, perhaps unpolished, but capable of the highest improvement. He would be an ignorant traveller who declared that there were no pearls in that vast expanse of water because unseen; equally ignorant, and still more uncharitable, he who denies the existence of good in the sailor. Rather let us pity his unfavourable condition, and employ agencies to ameliorate it, that we may hopefully anticipate the dawn of a new era upon the

purity of our maritime life. Thus we see manifested
in the appeal of this crew to Jonah—" What shall we
do unto thee ? "—the gentler side of a rough manhood.
There are times when to the most desperate life there
comes the pathos of deep submission ; and its advent
makes a sublime contrast to the degeneracy of former
days.

There is manifested in the conduct of this crew *a
true respect for God, which is shown by a kindly treatment of His Prophet.* They did not endeavour themselves to solve the problem of their woe, but uncon-
ditionally appealed to the judgment of Jonah. True
he had been detected in flight from God, but the crew
felt that there was yet a moral dignity lingering about
him which they could not explain, but which powerfully
crept over them, and bound them to him—hence, conscious that a Divine Presence was associated with him,
they paid that homage which it demanded. But perhaps we should not be right in attributing this outcome
of moral goodness from the mariners, more to the ordinary working of their nature, than to the dilemma into
which they had been cast by the storm. They knew
that the tempest was occasioned by God. They also
knew that Jonah was His Prophet. They, therefore,
feared to touch him. The wind was high and they
knew not how to subdue it. They consequently
appeal to Jonah that he may help them out of their
difficulty. This method of proceedure was *unusual.*
We do not often find when a man has been overtaken
in a fault, that his fellows ask him to determine his
penalty. Rather they make the imagined purity of his
prior life the subject of invective ; scandal is rife ;

vague reports are circulated ; and his companions leave him to the agony of solitude. Here these sailors become our pattern ; teaching us not to deal harshly, or unthinkingly with the guilty, driving them to despair ; but trying by kindness to awaken within them a feeling of true manhood, which may strengthen into yet more worthy character. This method of proceedure was also *magnanimous*. There are many natures so little that they cannot rise above the feeling of revenge; so crotchety that they can never overlook the petty annoyances of life; but this crew, outreaching the promptings of its lower nature, rose to a greatness of soul, which found expression in the language of this verse. If we had more of this magnanimity in our dealing with each other, life would be a very different thing from what it is now; its quarrels would be amicably settled; resentment would be calmed, and peace would throw a most potent charm over our otherwise restless hearts.

Finally, this verse teaches *the folly of delay when God demands the performance of unpleasant duty.* "For the sea wrought and was tempestuous." The tempest was the voice of God telling the mariners to cast Jonah overboard. They delayed. The storm becomes fiercer, and their situation more perilous. And such is always the case with those who tardily heed the indications of Divine Providence. When we are called upon to perform unpleasant duty in reference to the life, and well-being of another — although natural instinct may rebel, and a feeling of deep pity suggest reprieve—louder will grow the voice, articulating in darker tempest, its impatient demand. Then delay is dangerous, and may result in the death of many; whereas, if the first warning had been obeyed, the surrender of the guilty one, would have calmed the hurricane.

And he said unto them, Take me up, and cast me forth into the sea; so shall the sea be calm unto you: for I know that for my sake this great tempest is upon you.—*Verse* 12.

This verse contains *Jonah's reply to the inquiry of these perplexed mariners.* They had asked the Prophet what they were to do with him, that the sea might be calm unto them, and he tells them to cast him overboard. "Take me up, and cast me forth into the sea." This reply was *manly.* Had many people been placed in like circumstances, they would probably have commenced an elaborate apology, expressive of deep regret at the danger entailed by their conduct, and of a determination to amend for the future. Or they might have entered into a series of arguments, if the crew would have tolerated them, urging that the tempest would yet cease in a few moments; shewing the cruelty of death as the penalty of so light an offence, also its injustice as compared with the leniency manifested to them, who, though having spent their lives in heathen turpitude, would nevertheless be allowed to pursue their way unhurt; and likewise the apparent futility of murder to give the calm they wanted. No plea would have been too trivial; no device would have been too mean, to have been urged as an argument for reprieve. This reply was *submissive.* When Jonah said "Take me up and cast me forth into the sea," he did not mean that

he would rather die than go to Nineveh. It was not
the request of defiance, nor was it the utterance of
despair, but of holy resignation to the will of God.
We can easily imagine that Jonah might have acted
very differently from the way in which he did. He
might have used the new idea of God which had just
dawned upon the minds of these heathen men, as a means
of terror, and so have prevented injury to himself.
But no, he did not take unfair advantage of his Prophet position to impose upon the crew, to frighten their
superstition ; but he humbly placed himself as a man
on a level with them, and told them, at the expense of
his own life, to use the only remedy for safety. This
reply was also *deeply pathetic*. He tells this crew to
pursue a course which must result in his immediate
death. The past is unalterable. Its consequences are
upon him, and heroic action is demanded. Jonah rises
to the requirement of the hour, and becomes willing to
sacrifice his life for the safety of others. Surely, nothing could be more touching than this narrative. The
Prophet is overtaken in sin, and yet he urges these
men to open the portals of eternity before him. Had
Jonah repented of his flight from God? Was he ready
to meet that Being whom he had so wilfully denied ?
Yes, during the past few moments, in the silence of
his own heart, he had spoken to heaven for pardon.
It had come into his soul, and with it the power necessary to act in this noble manner. He requires not the
future for contrition, the present has sufficed ; and as
for reparation, he now offers it by his life. He is
ready to meet his God, and to go into the spirit world,
bearing at once the punishment of his sin, and also the

bright token of his victory over self. But God intends another destiny for Jonah; the Prophet's work is not completed yet; and, though a miracle be employed, his life must be spared.

This reply recognizes the truth that *man has no right to commit suicide.* Jonah did not throw himself into the sweeping waters, but told the crew to cast him forth; indicating that, although his death was a necessity, he dare not cause it himself. No circumstances however trying, no inducements however facinating, no arguments however logical, can justify a man in self-murder. No doubt there are times when life becomes a sad reality, pressing upon the mind with awful import; sin may have called into vigorous exercise all those influences which depress the human soul; the future is untrue, there is no principle of faith to bring it near, and hence the affrighted spirit is tempted to hush its unrest in the calm of a self-inflicted death. Bereavement may break asunder the dearest ties, and take the loved one from our heart; and fervent friendship, intensified by grief, may suggest the happiness of reunion in the world beyond the tomb. Or disaster occasioned by misplaced confidence, or commercial ruin, may robe life with every conceivable terror, until existence becomes a dreary journey to a long looked for peace, which no messenger of pain can disquiet. But no excuse however pathetic, no mad freak however frantic, can justify or even palliate self-murder. It entails alike the condemnation of God, and the horror of society. Then the question arises, would the sailors be right in obeying the command of Jonah, would they not become equally guilty of murder? Most certainly under ordinary circumstances; but now their unusual danger requires exceptional action. And, most likely, the reply of Jonah was not prompted by the sheer force of conscience, or by any mere presentiment that only his death could hush the tempest; but by a direct communication from God, telling him the course to be pursued; and, thus guided and strengthened by this mysterious revelation, Jonah informs the crew of their duty; and his character as a Prophet precludes all doubt as to the equity, and utility of the deed.

We behold in this verse *the reciprocal influence of moral character*. The crew had dealt generously with Jonah, and consequently made him wishful to act in a like manner to them. By their pity for, and sympathy with him, they had touched into exercise the more gentle feeling of his nature, until he becomes ready to die for their safety. We little know how potently we are influenced in our moral dispositions by the conduct of others towards us. If people in the every-day walks of life treat us respectfully, perhaps our pride may be flattered, or our knowledge of common etiquette may prompt us to a like return. But, if, on the other hand, we are treated with coldness or indifference, instead of manifesting a general flow of good feeling, our demeanour becomes haughty or else sternly conventional. As the effectiveness and pathos of music depend much upon the touch of the player; if the touch is heavy the melody will be harsh, but if gentle and well regulated, then the symphony will be refined. So if our hearts are struck by the unkind hand of impudence, the melody evoked is tumultous; but if the gentle finger of pity seeks the harmony of our nature, every note will

be clear and pathetic. Our mental and moral modes
depend much upon our companionships. In the company of certain men you cannot indulge in airs of
dignity; you cannot exhibit unkindness, their smiles
are so genial, their habits are so graceful, and their conduct so unconsciously spiritual, that their very presence
lifts the heaviest burden from you, gilds the dullest
hope with joy, and fills your entire being with delightful sympathy. So the manly dealing of these mariners
with Jonah excited like feelings within himself. If this
law of human intercourse was remembered, society
would get rid of half its petty annoyances, and would
be very much more happy in the enjoyments of its
pleasures.

What *an awful moment is that when a man awakes
to the fact that he is the medium of injury to his comrades.* Jonah here asserts his knowledge of this fact.
He assures the mariners that he has brought this peril
upon them—" For I know that for my sake this great
tempest is upon you." Many who stand in this relation
to their fellows are ignorant of it ; but how sad when
the man first awakes to the conviction that he has
introduced an element of sorrow into the life of another.
Well for him if in this awful crisis he has the moral
courage to confess his guilt, and to advise the only
remedy for its removal.

Who can imagine *the effects of these words upon the
mariners.* They had never heard the like before from
human lips, and they would wonder how Jonah could
have uttered them. Life was dear to them, and was
it not equally so to him ? had he no family whose
interests were wrapped up in himself ? had some terrible

disaster robbed life of its charm ?   No, the crew saw
that he was actuated by a Divine motive. They felt
that he was no ordinary man ; and that he was animated
by a holy power which they could not understand, but
which they instructively recognized as from God.

Nevertheless the men rowed hard to bring it to the land; but
they could not : for the sea wrought, and was tempestuous against
them.—*Verse* 13.

Truly, in this verse *we behold a sight of no ordinary
moral beauty*. The heathen mariners have heard the
manly confession of Jonah, and whatever may have
been their desire before, now they feel that to touch
such a life would be the highest profanity, which might
result in the deepest injury. Nor have they any wish
to injure the Prophet. His heroic conduct has charmed
them, and they are spell-bound. But their admiration
did not merely find expression in a sentimental reverie,
but in the most potent effort for his safety—" The men
rowed hard to bring the ship to the land." But in
vain. For louder grew the voice which demanded the
surrender of Jonah.

Hence we are taught *the utter uselessness of human effort when opposed to the Divine will*. Men are
frequently found in hostility to God, trying to oppose
Him by ingenious plans, or by undaunted energy.
Sometimes this antagonism is prompted by the most
criminal motive, which occasionally, as in the verse
before us, is the result of a well-meaning but ignorant zeal. We should remember that these sailors were
heathen, and consequently had not been taught the
deeper principles of Divine truth. They were guided

more by intuition than by external revelation. Hence
they did not wait to enquire the will of God in reference
to Jonah, but immediately acted upon the dictate of
natural feeling. To these mariners it would appear
wicked to take another man's life; so without looking
beneath the surface of things to find the unvarying
principle of right, they tried to row the Prophet to
land. There is much in moral conduct apparently
wrong, which in reality is right. The Divine Will is the
standard of all rectitude. Thus, principle is not always
in harmony with human instinct; nor is to be estimated
by external appearance. As its Divinity is often latent,
there must be a reverent inquiry into the inner meaning of the events through which we may be called to
pass, before there can be conduct righteously adapted
thereto. And in that the crew did not examine more
fully into the bearing of the tempest and its design,
consists their error. And this concealment of principle is made a means of moral discipline. It tests our
faith, and calls into exercise our knowledge of Divine
truth, which must be adapted to the exigencies of
human life. But we cannot justly criminate these
mariners for acting as they did; through lack of education, their spiritual perception was not sufficiently
quick to recognise in the storm the voice of God. And
not until Jonah had vocalised the inarticulate meaning
of the tempest, did they imagine that it required his
life.

*There are multitudes in the present day, but animated
by very different motives, acting the part of these heathen
mariners.* They have launched some great ship upon
the restless tide of human being; every influence

appears to hinder its progress. There is a Jonah on board, but still they row hard to bring him to land. Such is the case with the *unprincipled statesman,* who has cast his barque upon the ever changing waters of political thought. His ambition longs for a favourable gale to press it forward. But a tempest has arisen, which not only impedes its progress, but endangers its safety. His destined reform is not founded upon honest principle; its prompting motive is self-aggrandizement. And however diligent the effort of the crafty politician, God will not permit such a vessel to be rowed to land. The Jonah will have to be thrown overboard before the nation of such a man will prosper. *The dishonest tradesman* has also his ship floating upon the tide of commercial speculation. His one desire is to get wealth; how he cares not. Consequently he invents schemes by which he may dupe the public; and thus, by unwholesome adulteration and petty trickery, he endeavours to gratify his greed. But do not imagine that such a course can be carried on long without tempest. You have a Jonah on board; and if you do not mind you will be destroyed by the righteous anger of an avenging Deity. Only the vessel of the honest merchant will reach the shore of pure enjoyment.

For honesty hath many gains, and well the wise have known
This will prosper at the end, and fill their house with gold.
The phosphoros of cheatery will fade, and all its prophets perish,
While honesty with growing light endureth as the moon.
Yea, it would be wise in a world of thieves, where cheating were
    a virtue,
To dare the vice of honesty, if any would be rich :
For that which by the laws of God is heightened into duty,
Ever, in the practice of a man, will be seen both policy and
    privilege.

It may be that many who are listening to the teaching of this verse are in deep trouble; clouds and darkness are round about you; all your energy has been spent in a vain effort to gain relief. If such is the case, do not struggle with your difficulties; but calmly examine the motive of your life, and the meaning of your grief, that, brought into a contrite attitude of soul, you may receive Divine guidance.

Wherefore they cried unto the Lord, and said, We beseech thee, O Lord, we beseech thee, let us not perish for this man's life, and lay not upon us innocent blood : for thou, O Lord, hast done as it pleased thee.—*Verse* 14.

In the prayer of these mariners we have exhibited *a marvellous transition of moral character.* No one can tell the many changes which come over the moral history of every human life. Their nature is beyond prediction, and their number cannot be computed. As the river flows through a variety of scenery on its way to the ocean, so our souls, in their great march onward to the future, are frequently called upon to enter ever fluctuating experiences. Only a few minutes ago these sailors were praying to their heathen deities, but now they are crying to the true God. Surely this transition of character is *great and for the better.* Though, morally speaking, these mariners may have to commence life again; to remodel it according to the outline and beauty of a new ideal. Sorrowful as their task may be, and difficult as it will no doubt prove, it is a matter for joy that they are thus early, though probably late for many of them, convinced of its necessity. That they were not carried into the solemnity of an unlooked for hereafter, there to awake, for the first time, to the consciousness of a misspent life. Now they have opportunity to rectify the past; and from the fact that they are bowed in prayer, we behold as in the eastern sky, the first tinge of morning dawn.

We learn from this, *that God, in the mysterious arrangements of His providence, sends to the heathen means whereby they may be instructed in the truth.* No thoroughly organised Missionary Society had ever reached these men; no Prophet had been intentionally commissioned to unfold to them the truth. This result was apparently accidental. Jonah was not sent to them, but to the Ninevites; the tempest was not designed to interrupt their journey, but to arrest his flight, yet both the folly of the Prophet, and the raging of the storm, worked out the moral welfare of these mariners. How inexplicable does this page of history appear to us. It almost indicates that heathen minds are not left entirely untutored. True, the instruction given may be scanty, but still the light, though feeble, is sufficient to convince of darkness. And also to announce the nearness of a sun from which the flickering ray has come. Yes, probably many heathen, who we suppose have never heard the Gospel, may, after all, have listened to its tidings from the lips of a runaway, but penitent Prophet. God does not always work by societies, occasionally He employs means less conventional, making the most unlikely instrumentalities coincide with the purpose of His will.

Does not this page show *that the wickedness of man's free agency is overruled by God for the advance-*

ment of His cause. We cannot altogether impute the spiritual enlightenment of these men to Jonah, for it was not, in the first instance, contemplated by him. But we must ascribe it to that Being who had so wrought upon the heart of the disobedient Prophet that, contrary to his prior intention, yea even during the committal of sin, he became the means of their conversion. This transition of moral character was *rapid*. Only an hour ago these men were crying to their own gods, but now they worship the maker of the sea and the dry land. What is this but instantaneous conversion, at which so many people in these days are wont to sneer? And surely a very different example from those instances which occur around us in this Christian land. These men were heathen in their creed, maritime in their habits of life, and therefore the most unlikely to be the subjects of such a moral transformation. Therefore, if this rapid change of life was experienced by them, its possibility cannot be denied to us, whose history to begin with is not so dark, and whose external circumstances are much more favourable. Are we told that the transition of conduct manifested by these mariners was prompted more by a *selfish* desire for safety, than by a radical change of heart? This is not only a gratuitous, but an uncharitable assumption, which no one can be warranted in making. No doubt the crew had been frightened by their danger, but such feelings were only of temporary duration, and immediately yielded to the repose of truth. Had fear continued the most prominent impulse of their hearts, they could not have prayed, but would have cast forth Jonah at once into the sea. Had they acted as terror-

stricken heathen, selfishly seeking their own welfare,
this would have been the course adopted. But now
they are Christian; and so completely has their life
changed, so deeply spiritual has it become, and so
intensely pathetic, that its natural voice is that of
prayer. If then this plea of selfishness cannot be
maintained, are we told that such a transition of moral
character is *unnatural?* Is it asserted that the human
mind is not so susceptible of conversion; that there
must be a long period of investigation; and an intricate process of argument, before it can be induced to
abandon long accepted conclusions? No doubt this is
generally the case, but certainly not always. Most of
us are conscious of the possibility of sudden conviction.
How frequently have thoughts entered our mind entirely
uninvited, and in a moment they have changed the
intention of a year, and inaugurated new methods of
effort. These quick transitions are discernable in
nature. The weather changes in a moment from sunshine to shower. Now the sky is blue, again it is
overcast with darkness. At morning the flowers are
gay, while at evening they are withered. May we not,
therefore, conclude, that if such transitions are visible
in the realm of nature, that they are, to say the least,
not unlikely in the sphere of mind? Yes, every soul
has its moral April of fitful and alternate experiences.

Not only was this change of character rapid, *but it
was also unexpected by the mariners themselves.* Had
you told these hardy sailors upon commencing their
voyage, that before landing at their destined port, they
would all have abandoned the religion of their boyhood
for some unknown God; and that within a few hours,

instead of paying homage to their national idols, they would bow the knee to Jehovah — they would have probably laughed out a decisive sneer. And had they further been informed that the man in Prophet's garb, who has just come on ship-board, was to be the means of a change so wonderful —his presence would have been their constant joke, until the severity of the tempest would inspire a vague idea, that, after all, they might be on the eve of a spiritual crisis. How contrary then was this change of character to their expectation. And have not many of us had like experiences? Perhaps, while out one day on business, or engaged in one pursuit of pleasure, we casually entered a place of worship to hear some reputed minister; the Word reached our heart, and has issued in our conversion, in a manner totally unforseen. Instances of this kind are of daily occurrence, and but for its prejudice, the world would have become familiar with them long ago.

Further we are taught in this verse *the first attitude of a reformed life.* The mariners are engaged in prayer to Jehovah. So deep was their conviction, so real was their conversion, that they stood no longer in doubt, but at once gave the strongest evidence possible of their confidence in God. So it will ever be with any who may experience a like change. They will pray —and in their prayer gratitude will occupy the most prominent place, in that the Divine Being has aroused to a sense of error, before the solemn and unalterable realities of the future life had dawned upon them.

This prayer manifested *a sensitive disposition on the part of these mariners.* " And lay not upon us inno-

cent blood." They did not wish to destroy the life of
any man, much less of a Prophet, who had been the
medium of their spiritual good, and whose life was so
intimately associated with the Power of God. Did
they cast Jonah into the waters, they were afraid that
the remembrance of the fact would never leave them,
but that it would become the terror of their sleep, and
the constant attendant of their everyday thought. All
the natural instincts ef their souls rebelled against the
deed, and therefore to avoid the responsibility of its
committal, they pray to God that he will direct them to
the right.

The terms of this prayer are most natural and
affecting. *It contains an appeal to the Sovereignty of
God.* " For thou Lord hast done as it pleased thee."
The events of the last few hours had not altogether
been the result of their own conduct ; but had been
occasioned by the direct interposition of God for the
arrest of Jonah. Therefore these mariners cannot doubt
but that He will take the entire control of the tempest
until its full design shall have been accomplised. Hence
it becomes their duty to ascertain, and obey, the Divine
injunction. And if the death of Jonah is required,
they have nothing to do but throw him into the sea,
leaving the result with the Providence that commissioned the deed.

After all, it appears *almost incredible that the terror-
stricken men of the fifth verse are really the same whose
prayer now falls upon our ear.* What a wonderful
change has come over them ! You have seen that old
city at midnight ; but how little of its grandeur could
you discern ; simply the dim outline of its buildings

appeared to your vision. The next day at noon you
entered the very same streets, but how different
their aspect. Why? Because now you gaze upon them
in the sun-light. So, at the commencement of this
narrative, we met with these mariners clothed in the
darkness of idolatry. But now the light of an anticipated Christ shines upon them; and hence the beautiful change in their moral character. Oh! that upon
our lives, dark and unholy, there may come a beam of
light from the Cross, which gives to penitent human
nature the perfection of a Divine life.

We learn, lastly, *that these transitions of moral
character come upon us in proportion as we realize the
true meaning of the Divine existence.* These men had
just been brought into contact with the deep mystery
of God. Their hearts had found in Him the holy calm
they needed; hence the fervour of their prayers. Yes!
When the idea of God mingles for the first time with
the ordinary current of our souls, all within us is
quickened into new energy. And the individual character passes from the narrowness of river life, into the
vastness of an ocean existence. Waves of great ideas
sweep across its mental shores, being set in motion by
the supreme thought of God.

So they took up Jonah, and cast him forth into the sea; and the
sea ceased from her raging.—*Verse* 15.

Who can imagine the scene on board the vessel?
The crew are standing around the culprit Prophet.
Their prayers are ended. Their consultations are con-
cluded. The mariners can scarcely hold their footing

upon the deck of the reeling ship. The tempest is growing darker every moment, they, therefore, determine to commit Jonah to the custody of the mighty deep, until that eventful morning when the sea shall give up her dead. The seamen, with sad demeanour, bare the Prophet gently in their hands, and let him down into the restless waters. What a picture! No artist could have sketched it; imagination could not have reached its solemn beauty. There was no confusion on board. The sailors were calm in their disposition, and the on-lookers were silent in their grief. Truly, prayer had fitted all concerned to play their part in this unprecedented drama. No sooner had the Prophet disappeared beneath the waters than the storm ceased. The clouds parted. The sea became tranquil. And the delayed ship was allowed to pursue its onward journey. This immediate change in the elements would assure the seamen that they had performed their duty, and that the Divine blessing now rested upon them.

We gather from the conduct of these mariners *that extreme measures should not be resorted to until all others have failed.* These sailors had cast their wares overboard, had made use of the lot, and had tried prayer as a means of safety; but all these had hopelessly failed to quiet the tempest. Then, as a last and only resource, they threw Jonah into the sea. Had many of us been on board the ship, we should probably have suggested this remedy at the outset of the storm. Impatience would have prevented prayer, and anger would have unfitted for approach to God. But not so with the crew, and let us be instructed by their sensitive heroism in reference to Jonah. It may be that many here have need to learn this lesson. Probably some unfortunate man has for a long time received goods from you on credit, until now his debt reaches a large amount of money, which he feels it impossible to pay. In order to support his family comfortably, and carry on his business hopefully, he requires all the capital at his disposal. If such is the case, learn from this crew not to employ harsh measures against him all at once. Strive by milder intimations of the law, to regain your due, and do not resort to its last extremity until the former have failed. And, even when severity is needful, imitate the example of these sailors who prayerfully executed, yet sorrowfully lamented that they were called upon to undertake so painful a duty.

This verse also teaches *the equity of God's dealings with mankind.* "And the sea ceased from her raging." Directly the mariners had cast Jonah overboard, God gave them the calm they needed. And so it is now. As the punishment came through sin, so when the evil is repented of and abandoned, mercy will dawn through the tempest in all its beauty. God does not punish us immoderately, but according to the most rigid law of necessity, and, therefore, when the Jonah of our moral life is left behind in our progress to the future—God causes the sea to cease from her raging.

Then the men feared the Lord exceedingly, and offered a sacrifice unto the Lord, and made vows.—*Verse* 16.

Seldom have men anywhere been called to witness, in so short a time, such a series of wonders. The deed is done. In all likelihood the Prophet is dead long before this; and this fear of the mariners is the respect they

pay to his memory. They could not but regard him
favourably, for although he had done them injury, it
had been far outweighed by the religious feeling which
he had instrumentally awakened within them. All
through life they would experience the benefit of Jonah's
teaching. But now he is dead. They would not
more be able to repay his kindness, or to show their
appreciation of his manly conduct. He is for ever
beyond their reach. But, nevertheless, they will not
be able to forget him. His name will be for ever
written upon their hearts—and, therefore, now they
pay it the homage of a reverent fear. And can we
wonder, after such extraordinary experiences, that this
crew should fear the Lord? After the death of so
remarkable a man, and after the unprecedented event
by which it had been followed, in the immediate calm
that came upon the tempest, they felt more than ever
that the newly found Deity was indeed "the God of
heaven which hath made the sea and the dry land."

Here we learn *that where there is holy feeling it will
be manifested by the performance of religious worship.*
"And offered a sacrifice, and made vows." We cannot tell the nature of the sacrifice offered on this occasion. Nor is it a matter of importance that we should;
the fact contains the lesson for us, and that is sufficient.
Perhaps they had a few animals remaining which had
not been cast overboard, or the offering may have con-
sisted in the sacrifice of God, which is a penitent and
a contrite heart. And as to the nature and extent of the
vows offered, at this time, we are equally in ignorance.
No doubt gratitude would be the most prominent sentiment of their hearts, and, in return for their late deliver-

ance, they might promise the homage and service of their
future lives, which vows we cannot doubt would be
most faithfully kept.   The mysterious circumstances
which had called them forth, and the solemnity of the
time at which they were uttered, together with the
tokens by which they were noted, would for ever
exclude the possibility of forgetfulness.   And thus the
ship which had so recently been the scene of a Prophet's
funeral, is now the place of most hallowed worship.
Have we not here a pattern for ourselves ?   Has not
God wrought out for us numerous deliverances; and
ought they not to have excited within us deep religious
emotion?   And how can we better express it than by
Christian worship ?   Worship is the natural outcome
of Godly fear; and if our lives are not marked by contrite hom age, it is a certain proof that our gratitude,
for help, in time gone by, is but feeble.   Let all who
accept the kindly Providence of God with thankless
hearts; who receive His mercy thoughtlessly, and who
habitually despise, or occasionally neglect, the sanctuary
of holy worship, find their reproof in the prayer, and
vows of these converted mariners.

Now the Lord had prepared a great fish to swallow up Jonah.
And Jonah was in the belly of the fish three days and three nights.
—*Verse* 17.

Now we come to *the miracle of Jonah being swallowed alive by the fish*, which has excited so much controversy.   Why this has been the case we are totally
at a loss to explain; for, humanly speaking, one miracle is as improbable as another, and the criticism which
rejects this, must if consistent also deny the rest which

are found in the record of inspired truth. No doubt
many unfriendly strictures have been awakened by the
somewhat *grotesque* character of this miracle. When
we are told that Christ opened the eyes of a blind man,
there is something in such a miracle with which we
heartily sympathize, and it accomplishes a purpose
which we cannot but commend. But when we are informed that a drowning man is *swallowed* and saved
alive by a fish, such a narrative is more calculated to
excite our laughter, than to win our admiration. The
moment that the story reaches us, we commence to
think about some Grecian legend, or Popish fabrication,
or it may be of Æsop's Fables. And, as people are
generally sensitive on the humourous side of their
nature, when a great truth comes clad in a somewhat
childish form, they are either in danger of denying its
reality, or of treating it with cold contempt. Such, to
a great extent, has been the case with the miracle
recorded in this verse. Like our blessed Lord, it has
been despised because of its common apparel; men
have not had the power of soul to look beneath the
outer garment for the evidences of supernatural worth.

Admitting, then, that the plainly woven texture of
the fact covers a miracle of royal instruction, *it
becomes us to approach it with caution and reverence.*
Many zealous writers have almost shown a disposition
to invest infidel objection with greater authority
than otherwise it could have acquired, by meeting it
half-way. The sceptic denies this to be a miracle, and
Christian writers have virtually agreed with him by
endeavouring to explain it, and by trying to distinguish
between the miraculous, and non-miraculous portion of

the narrative. This also has had a tendency to prolong the cavil, as ultimately the controversy has been removed from the scripture record, into the realms of scientific thought, where the supreme authority of God's Book has been either ignored or forgotten. To explain a miracle is an impossibility, and nothing pleases infidelity better than for us to make the attempt; because, if successful, the Christian writer just proves what the sceptic has declared, that it is not a miracle, else it could not have been so easily unfolded. There is, and ever must be, a Divine mystery about the miracles of God's Word, which can never be penetrated by the eye of human reason. Into that Holy of Holies we cannot go, we must stand without the veil, and even to try to draw aside the curtain would be the highest profanity. God moves there in his Divinest Presence, and it becomes us to adore, and not investigate. We must remember that the men of Bethshemesh were smitten because they looked into the ark of the Lord; and anyone trying to explain, or account for the mircales of God, is guilty of a like presumption, and may be visited with as terrible a calamity.*

In this spirit of true adoration we will proceed with the history, that we may gather the lesson it teaches. *Read carefully the words by which this miracle is described,* and this will fortify you against one great objection, which only ignorance could have suggested. Men have urged that a whale could not have swallowed Jonah, owing to the littleness of its throat; be that as it may, the narrative does not assert that he was so caught up. It says that "The Lord had prepared *a*

---

*1 Samuel 6:19

great fish" to swallow up Jonah. And objectors, wilfully, or through ignorance, have in their ordinary talk
substituted the individual for the genus, until no
doubt, many who have not carefully looked at the matter, fully believe that Jonah was imprisoned within a
whale.*

---

* Jonah speaks only of a *great fish*. The Greek word by which
the LXX. translated it, and which our Lord used, is, (like our " ceta-
cea," which is taken from it,) the name of a genus, not of any individual fish. It is, the equivalent of the *great fish* of Jonah. The
Greeks use the adjective as we do, but they also use the substantive
which occurs in S. Matthew. This designates a class which *includes*
the whale, but is never used to designate the whale. In Homer it
includes " dolphins and the dog." In the natural historians, (as Ari-
stotle,) it designates the whole class of sea-creatures which are vivi-
parous, " as the dolphin, the seal, and the whale ; " Galen adds the
zygæna (as shark) and large tunnies ; Photius says that " the Car-
charias, or white shark, " is a species of it." Oppian recounts, as
belonging to the Cete, several species of sharks and whales, some
with names of land animals, and also the black tunnies. Ælian
enumerates most of these under the same head. Our Lord's words
then would be rendered more literally *in the fish's belly*, than *in the
whale's belly*. Infidels seized eagerly on the fact of the narrowness
of the whale's throat ; their cavil applied only to an incorrect render-
ing of modern versions. Fish of such size that they can swallow a
man whole, and which are so formed as naturally to swallow their
prey whole, have been found in the Mediteranean. The white shark,
having teeth merely incisive, has no choice, except between swallow-
ing its prey whole, or cutting off a portion of it. It cannot *hold* its
prey, or swallow it piece-meal. Its voracity leads it to swallow at
once all which it can. Hence, Fabricus relates, "its wont is to swallow down dead, and, sometimes, also, living men, which it finds
in the sea.

A natural historian of repute relates, "In 1758, in strong weather
a sailor fell overboard from a frigate in the Mediteranean. A shark
was close by, which, as he was swimming and crying for help, took
him in his wide throat, so that he forthwith disappeared. Other
sailors had leapt into the sloop, to help their comrade, while yet swim-

Consider now *the agency by which this miracle was
wrought*. "Now the Lord had prepared a great fish."
This statement ought to put an end to all controversy.
All difficulty should be forgotten in communion with
Him whose Presence now shines in the unburnt bush.
Are we told that Jonah could not live in the stomach
of a fish; that there would be no warmth to preserve,
or food to nourish him? To these, and all kindred
enquiries, we reply that "the Lord had prepared a
great fish to swallow up Jonah." When a house is

---

ming; the captain had a gun which stood on the deck discharged at
the fish, which struck it so, that it cast out the sailor which it had in
its throat, who was taken up, alive and little injured, by the sloop
which had now come up. The fish was harpooned, taken up on the
frigate, and dried. The Captain made a present of the fish to the
sailor who, by God's Providence, had been so wonderfully preserved.
The sailor went round Europe exhibiting it. He came to Franconia,
and it was publicly exhibited here in Erbangen, as also at Nurnberg
and other places. The dried fish was delineated. It was 20 feet long, and,
with expanded fins, nine feet wide, and weighed 3924 pounds. From
all this, it is probable that this was the fish of Jonah.

In all modern works on Zoology, we find 30 feet given as a common length for a sharks body. Now a shark's body is usually only
about eleven times the length of the half of its lower jaw. Consequently a shark of 30 feet would have a lower jaw of nearly six
feet in its semicircular extent. Even if such a jaw as this was of
hard bony consistence instead of a yielding cartilagious nature, it
would qualify its possessor for engulphing one of our own species
most easily. The power which it has, by virtue of its cartilaginous
skeleton, of stretching, bending, and yielding, enables us to understand how the shark can swallow entire animals as large, or larger,
than ourselves.

Such facts ought to shame those who speak of the miracle of
Jonah's preservation through the fish, as a thing less credible than
any other of God's miraculous doings.—*Pusey on the Minor Prophets,
page* 257.

built for human habitation, no one questions the possibility of living in it, because it has been erected for that very purpose; and did not God equally *prepare* this fish to become the temporary residence of Jonah in the sea? And this very fact that the great fish was designed, by a Divinely competent authority, for such a purpose, should be a sufficient refutation of all sceptical objections.

The author of a book entitled "Can we believe in Miracles?"* in trying to prove that miracles are not violations of natural law, gives utterance to the following language in reference to the imprisonment of Jonah within the stomach of the great fish. He says, (page 122), "One case alone remains where the assertion of law being violated has some show of plausibility; that, namely, of the preservation of Jonah in the fish's belly for three days. Surely, it may be said, it is a law of human life that respiration is essential to continued existence; and how could respiration possibly have gone on in the stomach of a fish? True; *but then what warrant have we for saying that it did?* The whole of what scripture tells us on the point is (1) that Jonah was swallowed up alive, (2) that he was cast out alive, and (3) that he was aware of what went on during the interval. It is our inference merely that he was alive (in a bodily sense) during the interval. The language of Scripture, which everywhere speaks of personality as belonging to the soul, not to the body, in no way requires such bodily life; while there is much, both in the prayer of Jonah, and in the New Testament refer-

---

*Published under the auspices of the Christian Evidence Committee of the Society for Promoting Christian Knowledge.

cnces to the miracle, which points to bodily death as having, in fact, intervened. Thus regarded, the miracle* becomes one, among many others, of resurrection, and all *peculiar difficulty* is at an end." Such are the sentiments of our author. We are inclined to think that a defence of this kind is far from being helpful to the cause of Christian truth. For it is little better than a quibble. Whether we regard this miracle in the light of a preservation from death, or as a resurrection from the dead, it is equally inexplicable; and the latter supposition is as contrary to the operation of natural law as the former. Therefore, the writer gains nothing by such an argument. We want more fully to understand that miracles do not oppose the ordinary working of general law, but simply lead it into a realm of effort, for the accomplishment of moral purpose. Hence their supernatural character. Again we cannot agree with our auther that there is any " peculiar difficulty " involved in the preservation of Jonah, when we remember the Divine agency by which it was wrought.

But we wish more especially to direct your attention to his remark, *that the miracle here recorded is in reality a resurrection from the dead*. This we can never admit. Does not the narrative warrant us in saying that the point of the miracle lay in the preservation of Jonah from death, under such unheard of circumstances? True, the history does not tell us, in so many words, that he continued to live in the great fish, but it unmistakably implies that such was the case. In the parable of the Rich Man, which we may suppose, on very good evidence, to be real history, we are not

*Jonah 2:2-6, Matthew 12:39-40

directly informed of the burial of Lazarus. Yet, surely, no one could be found who would be foolish enough to doubt the fact. His interment is understood as a necessary consequence of his death. So the narrative, in reference to Jonah implies with equal certainty, that he continued to live after being cast overboard. It asserts that he was swallowed alive, and vomited up; and pray what more natural inference can be drawn, considering the Divine agency, than that he lived within the belly of the great fish. To assert that this is only predicated of his body, is a quibble unworthy of notice. But admitting, for the sake of argument, that the Prophet died, *we ask, where did his spirit go?* Are we told that it went to Heaven? But if so, why did he pray? Surely, as a member of that holy community, he would have no trouble from which to obtain relief. The language of his prayer is totally incompatible with any such conjecture. Then, if his spirit did not go to Heaven, are we warranted in thinking that it went to Hell? Most certainly not, as there he would not have prayed at all. Supplication would have been useless. And the petitions found in the next chapter could have no meaning but that of mockery. "Then I said, I am cast out of thy sight; yet I will look again toward thy holy temple."* Could this have been the cry of a lost soul? The Rich Man, in the parable just alluded to, uttered a prayer from hell, but it was merely for the alleviation of his torment, and not for its entire removal. He knew well enough that such an application would be in vain. But how different the spirit and language of Jonah's appeal, from the despairing utter-

---

*Jonah 2:4

ance of this tormented epicure. Yes ! it was uttered
amid vastly different scenes. Jonah had not yet entered
the spirit world. After being cast overboard, he felt
that life still remained to him ; that by some mysterious
power the death anticipated had been averted ; hence
finding that his case was not altogether hopeless, probably thinking that He who had hitherto protected,
would achieve for him a final deliverance—he commenced to pray. This is the most natural explanation
that can be given of his prayer written in the next
chapter. Again, we think that the petulance* which
Jonah manifested, when the Divine forgiveness was
extended to the Ninevites, is an unanswerable proof
that he had never experienced the awful reality of the
future life, or he would not have grieved that so large
a nation had been turned aside from it, when in such a
desperate condition of heart. And if this miracle was
a resurrection, why are we not told so, as in the other
cases reported in the Scripture ? Did the inspired
writer wish to deceive us ? Does not the Prophet
describe his experiences while in the belly of the fish ;
and how could he do this if he had not lived there ?
Thus we cannot accept the comment of the Author
just quoted. Remembering the agency by which this
miracle was wrought, we talk not of difficulty, or
natural law, but of God, and thus calmly receive the
narrative of His servant in all the simplicity and entirety of its meaning. "And Jonah was in the belly
of the fish three days and three nights." Nothing can
be more straightforward than this ; and nothing more
self-evident to a candid mind. True, we admit that

---

*Jonah 4:1

Christ died, and that Jonah was a type of our Saviour
in many important respects; but we cannot argue from
the antitype to the type, neither can we make similarities where there are none. Therefore let us credit the
narrative as written, and believe in the future, as we
have done in the past, that God in the exercise of His
Power, and in the order of His Providence, preserved
Jonah *alive* in the belly of the great fish.

We have so far contemplated the words by which
the miracle is described, the agency by which it was
wrought, we now invite your attention *to the benevolent
tendency by which it was distinguished.* You must not
view this miracle as merely working out the safety of
one human being. True, men were numerous enough
then as now, but Prophets were not. The benefit of
this miracle did not terminate with Jonah, but must be
regarded in its bearing towards the Ninevites, and the
age in which he lived. Any instrumentality that saves
the life of a Prophet is promotive of public good.
And especially would such be the case in the days of
which we speak, when the ministers of God were like
the few stars observable on a dark night, just illumina-
ting the darkness they try in vain to dispel. Or, to
pass rapidly to another figure, as the flower contains
the germ of future plants, so the spiritual good of the
Ninevites, together with the eternal welfare of men
unborn, were wrapt up in this marvellous continuance
of the Prophet's life.

How very simple is the record of this miracle. "Now
the Lord had prepared a great fish to swallow up Jonah.
And Jonah was in the belly of the fish three days and
three nights." How plain is the narrative. We find

no rhetorical embellishment here. There is no great effort on the part of the writer to indicate the presence of anything extraordinary. Jonah himself makes no boast at having been the hero of such a wonderful history. Had some men have passed through a like experience without injury, they would have made it the staple talk of their lives, if not the special theme of some brilliant book. Jonah, however, allows the stream of his narrative to run on in calmness, as though nothing unusual had happened to break it into a ripple. He felt that the miracle had been wrought by a supernatural agency, and that therefore any display, or excitement in the narration thereof, would not only be unnatural, but also unholy. It was no more difficult for God thus to have kept him alive, than for the mariners to have cast their wares into the sea, or for them to have prayed for relief. Hence, regarding the miracle from this, its proper standpoint, he continues the record in the unadorned language of the former verses.

Before we go on to the more practical teaching of this verse, we cannot but express our belief that *there is a growing tendency, in many congregations, to discredit the miracles of Scripture.* We appear to think that they are mythical; or, we regard them as interpolations which have no right in the Bible. We regret that this kind of criticism has a place in our Christian churches. It cannot but result in great spiritual injury. True, the peculiar age of miracles is past. We do not see them now, and therefore try to persuade ourselves that they were probably never wrought. We have no need for miracles in our times. For a long time after the husbandman has planted the sapling tree, he waters, and tends it carefully ; but in the lapse of months, when it has gathered stability, he leaves it to grapple alone with the tempest. So Christianity, when first introduced to the world, required the ministry of miracles to establish its doctrinal authority. But this being attained, its object was accomplished, and the visible manifestation of Christly Power was merged in the unseen agency of the Holy Spirit. If therefore any man wishes to overcome, what we cannot but call the sceptical mental habit of the present day, let him hold unbroken communion with the Holy Spirit ; then all doubt, about the possibility of miracles, will soon be lost in those rich influences which ever come from His sacred Presence.

We gather from this narrative *how kindly God alleviates the punishment of contrite offenders.* If the Prophet had not manifested a holy penitence for his past unfaithfulness, he might have been given over to the awful extremity of death. But seeing that he has acted, during the last few hours, with such Christian resignation and promptitude, God, in token of benediction, mitigates his peril, and ultimately delivers him from it. True, repentance is not always followed by so happy an issue ; though, when linked to Christ by earnest faith, it may command pardon, yet it is not of necessity a harbinger of release from the effect of prior crime. It may be that the repentant one has indulged so long in habits of intemperance, that the germs of consumption are scattered broadcast within him. In all likelihood God will not put forth his hand to uproot, but may permit them to ripen into the grim fruit of death. For in the Divine method of procedure, punishment is quite compatible with pardon. We read,

" Thou answeredst them, O Lord, our God: thou wast a God that forgavest them, though thou tookest vengeance of their inventions." * But even in anticipated death, repentance would alleviate his grief, for instead of being frantic with despair, like the man whose little boat is being carried on the rapids, without rudder to guide, or oar to prevent advancement to the terrible Niagara, the roar of whose waters now strikes upon him like the voice of thunder. Instead of this, he gathers the joy of the hopeful mariner, who after a long voyage of tempest, beholds in the distance the haven towards which he tends, bathed in the calm of declining evening. To what, under such circumstances of bodily decay, can we attribute his spiritual composure, but to that transformation of character, which has come upon him, through faith in the death of Christ?

Further, we learn *that God sometimes employs the most unlikely means for the safety of the good.* In fact, most people are astonished that the Divine Being should have commissioned a fish to become the guardian of a Prophet. They are ready to think it *beneath the dignity of God* to have taken advantage of such an agency for the purpose. We venture to suggest, however, that, under the circumstances, it was the most natural that could possibly have been chosen. The mariners were upon the mighty deep, and Jonah being cast into it, if saved at all, what more likely method could, humanly speaking, have been adopted? True, it was humiliating to the Prophet, but it was much more than he either expected or deserved. However, we must not look merely at the great fish, but at its association with

---

*Psalm 99:8

the Divine Purpose, and then all thought of indignity will immediately vanish. The meanest instrumentality is lifted from its ordinary sphere of value when touched by the hand of God ; that very touch transforming a shark into the home of a Prophet, yea even into a temple of prayer. How often have good people been delivered from imminent peril by the timely providence of God; and by expedients equally unlikely as this now under review. When Prophets, and folk of kindred character, are saved from death, all criticism, as to the agency by which it has been achieved, should be forgotten in that overwhelming gratitude, whose only utterance is praise. For not merely is a life preserved to the world, but lofty thoughts, holy emotions, and Christly instruction, which will be beneficial to mankind, when their saintly author shall have yielded to the irrevocable decree of an unrescued death.

Lastly, we learn from this verse *that some men have a twofold history*. By the mariners Jonah would be thought of as drowned. Whereas he was still living. Frequently have we met with this kind of thing in the tragedies of sensational novels. Heroes, whom all have supposed dead, unknown to their friends have been wonderfully rescued, only to pursue a life of continued adventure, until an unexpected circumstance has brought them face to face with the companions of their youth. But the narrative of Jonah, even in this apparent similarity, differs from fiction, both in the style of its composition, and also as to the motive by which its author was animated. Here we have nothing extravagant. The design of the history is not to awaken a mere feeling of interest, but to excite the highest

reverence for the Providence of God. We are not told
whether these mariners ever met with Jonah again. On
this matter the narrative is silent. They thought him
dead, and therefore would very reluctantly credid any
rumour announcing him to be living. Perhaps they may
have heard about him in connection with the national
humiliation and repentance of the Ninevites. The
sailors would know that Nineveh was his destination,
and that his mission thither was to denounce its
wickedness. They also knew that Jonah was associated
with the Power of God, and that therefore his life may
have been miraculously preserved. This consideration
might shake their belief in his death. But if any of
them did meet with the Prophet, how glad would be
the greeting; what tidings would each have to communicate; surely nothing could have severed a friendship thus renewed.

We now come to the conclusion of this chapter.
In it we have formed the most intimate and beneficial
friendships. For, after all, Jonah is a man we cannot
fail to admire; and as for the mariners they have gained
upon us in proportion as we have come to know them
more fully. In reference to them we would heartily
re-utter the sentiments of a valuable writer* on this
subject. "If I were making a voyage I could ask for
no readier hands to furl or spread the sail—for no truer
hearts in every time of need or danger. I could wish
for no better captain—supposing, of course, that he

---

*Alexander Raleigh, *The Story of Jonah the Prophet.*

shall have the modern scientific knowledge—than he
who looked so well to the ship, and roused the sleepers
to their prayers." And thus these men whom we met
with an indifferent shake of the hand, we now take
leave of with a thousand regrets that we cannot longer
enjoy their instructive company. We leave all the
characters of the chapter much better than we found
them, and we hope that they will leave us better than
when we first made their acquaintance. Our mental
companionships exert as potent an influence over us
as our bodily. Let us, therefore, endeavour to obtain
eternal good from our transient intercourse with these
seamen. Certainly, they have inculcated many truths
worthy of our study. They have taught us lessons, the
importance of which can never be overrated, and the
effect of which, upon our eternal destiny, will only be
made known at the last great day.

*Before, however, finally leaving this chapter we will
briefly review it as a whole, just gathering its most prominent teaching.* True, each verse is a diamond refulgent
with light; but now we can view the entire setting,
both in its finished design and chaste beauty.

We see illustrated in this chapter more especially
*the marvellous Providence of God in its bearing upon
moral character.* We learn here that all the tempestuous events of human life, whether occasioned by our
sin or folly, are intended for the discipline of our
souls, that purified by Divine influences they may be
brought into harmony with the Will of God. Hence,
when the night is dark, when the sea is rough, when
the track is difficult to discern, look not at the surging
waters, but at the clear star shining above. That

star is the Providence of God, which appears bright
amid the darkest storm, to the praying spirit.

*This Chapter also brings out beautifully the doctrine
of prayer, as offered by ignorant, but well meaning men.*
Men can only act according to the knowledge they
possess, and, in so doing, in a mysterious manner, they
respond to an unknown, but Divine claim resting upon
them. At this point, their prayers are met by the
mediation and intercession of Christ, which cannot but
impart to them a fragrance acceptable to God. No
one can plead ignorance as an argument for neglecting
prayer. All men pray, if not to God, yet to the moon
or stars. Prayer is generally acknowledged to be a
duty,—the difference between us and the heathen is in
the object to whom it is be presented. Thus when
the untutored pagan finds that his idols are deaf to his
voice, his heart begins to cry out, however feebly, yet
truly, for the Divine Parent. Then are we not justified
in believing that the mediatorial work of Christ gives to
such an outcry for peace, the spirit and efficacy of
prayer? Do not the verses which we have contemplated
intimate as much?

*This Chapter also shows the powerful influences which
frequently come upon men in the performance of their
everyday work.* The men whose conversion from idolatry is here narrated gained their livelihood as seamen.
And while on a voyage in the Mediterranean sea they
hear for the first time about the true God. And has
not the dull monotony of our everyday toil frequently
been broken in upon by the instruction of some Pro-
phet-thought, or by the bright effulgence of another
world. And, perhaps, from that very moment we date

our change of heart.   Every avenue of our life is open
to the presence of God.

*We desire now to invite your attention to the narra-
tive of Jonah as typical, in certain respects, of the history
of Christ.* And, in order that we may bring out this coin-
cidence more clearly before you, also that we may have
the opportunity of a more immediate reference to Evan-
gelical truth, *we shall note a few important features in the
mission of Jonah which do not find their counterpart in
that of Christ.* We find that Jonah ran away from the
Divine commission, whereas Christ gladly accepted
it. When the Word of the Lord came to Jonah telling
him to go to Nineveh, he arose and took ship for Tarshish. On the contrary, when the Divine method of
salvation was propounded, which involved the incarna-
tion and death of the second Person in the Holy
Trinity, Christ exclaimed, "Lo, I come (in the volume
of the book it is written of me) to do thy will, O
God."* There was no delay through unwillingness.
The most cheerful promptitude was at once manifested.
Thus, while in the flight of Jonah, we behold the weakness of human nature; in the cheerful obedience of
Christ we see the unerring rectitude of his Divine
life.

Another point of contrast is seen in the fact that
Jonah deserved the punishment that came upon him;
*while the death of Christ, not occasioned by personal folly,
was totally unmerited.* The Prophet had, as the consequence of disobedience, involved himself in guilt,
and his companions in danger, hence when the mariners threw him into the sea, they did but perform a

*Hebrews 10:7

duty which God had rendered necessary to their own
safety. Not so with our blessed Saviour. Not once
do we find throughout his unparalleled career, that
he endangered the well-being of another through
personal delinquency. On the contrary, he never came
into association with men without throwing upon
them the brightness and joy of His own Divine Spirit.
In His presence sin was forgiven, health was restored,
and men long dead were brought from the darkness of
the grave to the charm and affection of domestic life.

Thus, if we contemplate the contrast between the
life of Jonah and that of Christ, we must admit that
as the former deserved death, the latter, at least,
merited the warmest sympathy of those by whom
he was surrounded. But, instead of this, they crucified
him. And thus the man whose life, like a violet
upon the dusty road-side, gave forth a fragrance to the
traveller, was cut down like a poisonous herb. Think
about this fact. Learn from it the ingratitude of
man. See in it the deep mystery of that God who,
" so loved the world, that he gave his only begotten
Son, that whosoever believeth in him should not perish,
but have everlasting life."*

Having viewed the broad lines of dissimilarity which
exist between the mission of Jonah and that of Christ;
we will now direct your attention to the points in which
the former is typical of the latter. *Christ, like Jonah, was
the means of holy instruction to those by whom he was
surrounded.* Jonah for the first time informed the
mariners of the true God, and but for him they might
have remained in darkness to the end of their days.

*John 3:16

So Christ has communicated to us a knowledge of all those higher truths, which are so necessary to our eternal welfare; and but for Him, mankind would have been left in ignorance for ever. The most memorable scenes in the time of our Lord are those which refer to Him in company with the ignorant and doubtful. Never will the world forget His evening conversation with the Jewish Councillor, or His noontide meeting with the woman of Samaria. No! the narrative is indelibly written upon the universal heart of man. It exhibits a beauty beyond comparison, and contains a charm which no language can express. Christ is the light of the intellectual and moral world. The rays streaming from Him are so penetrating that they can illumine the most untutored mind, and touch into vigour the most indolent spirit. He not only revealed to men the doctrines which they were to believe, but also the principle according to which they should live. Hence His instruction was of deep spiritual tendency, and found abundant exemplification in the perfection of His own life. But, though Jonah and Christ resemble each other in the fact that both were the means of instruction to others, they differ widely as to the circumstances under which it was given. Jonah taught the mariners as a disobedient but repentant Prophet, while Christ educated the people as the unerring Son of God.

Again, *the casting of Jonah into the sea, like the death of Christ, was for the safety of others.* If the Prophet had not been thrown overboard, the whole crew would have been drowned. So if Christ had not died, the entire world, overtaken by the storm of Divine vengeance, must have perished with a terrible ruin. Whereas, now we are not only allowed to prosecute the duties of life with success, but have also inspired within our hearts the hope of an eternal calm beyond the grave.

Further, *the supposed death of Jonah was similar in its effects to the death of Christ.* Directly the Prophet was cast into the sea the elements " ceased from their raging," and the mariners began immediately to thank God for their deliverance. So when Christ is brought into sympathetic contact with the human soul, all the disquiet of its passion is hushed, and the agitation of its unsatisfied hope is immediately calmed. The only way to subdue the tempest of the world's passion is to let Christ down into its seething waters. And not until this is done will there come upon the tumultous nations of the earth the calm they need. Again, as the supposed death of Jonah was succeeded by the prayers of the crew, so the sacrifice of Christ upon the Cross will one day be followed by the homage of universal man.

Further, *the temporary confinement of Jonah in, and his final deliverance from the belly of the great fish is typical of the burial and resurrection of our Saviour.* When thrown into the sea the Prophet would be considered by the mariners as irrevocably lost to them ; equally would the Disciples regard the burial of Christ as a dark token of life-long separation. True, He had unfolded to them the fact of His resurrection, but they had not understood it, and therefore had no bright hope to chase away the melancholy forbodings that came upon them. Again, we can easily imagine that the tidings of

Jonah's wonderful deliverance, reaching the Ninevites, would become to them a proof of the reality of his mission. Equally should the resurrection of Christ from the dead authenticate His claims to a world-wide service, and establishes, beyond denial, the Divine acceptance of His life-work.

———

Although we have advanced so far in the history of our Lord, *we must not conclude this exposition without comparing the sleep of Jonah, recorded in this chapter, with that of Christ in the little ship, during the tempest upon the lake.* " But the Lord sent out a great wind into the sea, and there was a mighty tempest in the sea, so that the ship was like to be broken. Then the mariners were afraid, and cried every man unto his god, and cast forth the wares that were in the ship into the sea, to lighten it of them. But Jonah was gone down into the sides of the ship; and he lay, and was fast asleep." (Jonah i. 4—5.) " And, behold, there arose a great tempest in the sea, insomuch that the ship was covered with the waves : but he was asleep." (Matt. viii. 24.) From this comparison we learn *that storms overtake good men in the performance of duty, as well as disobedient in the neglect of it.* They are a means of holy discipline whereby, like the timorous disciples, we being awakened to a consciousness of our weakness, are driven to Christ for help. The tempest also gives an opportunity for the manifestation of Divine Power, and during such times we generally get new revelations of God, so that our hearts exclaim, " What manner of man is this, that even the winds and the sea obey him." *

We further see *that good men appear to better advantage in storms than the disobedient.* Christ, by a word, hushed the elements, and also inspired moral courage into the hearts of His companions; while Jonah, impotent himself, became the inspiration of terror to others. The good man always commands the fury of circumstances, making them an occasion for the exercise of moral power. But the disobedient, in the difficulties of life are like the broken wreck, floating upon the ocean, tossed by every wind, and carried upon the crest of every wave.

Lastly, we learn from this common sleep, *that both the good and the bad are under the same law of physical life.*† Sleep, being the law of our nature, is independent of moral character. Jonah slept through exhaustive grief, and Christ from the fatigue of benevolent work. Hence we have two widely differing experiences issuing in apparently the same result. Both men are unconscious of danger, one is prepared for it, and the other is not. However, soon they awake, and then we behold the weakness of the one, and the might of the other. The awakening is the index to their slumber. Oh that our nightly repose may always be as peaceful, and when the final storm of life breaks upon us, then may our death-sleep be as calm as was the Saviour's on the deck of this little vessel—so that we may awake in that realm where the mutter of storm is unheard, where there is no more sea.

---

*Matthew 8:27
†See Editor's Series of the Homilist, vol. 2, page 193.

Though waves and storms go o'er my head,
Though strength, and health, and friends be gone,
Though joys be withered all and dead,
Though every comfort be withdrawn ;
On this my steadfast soul relies :
Father, thy mercy never dies.

" Call upon me in the day of trouble : I will deliver thee, and
thou shalt glorify me."—Psalm 1:15

JONAH 2

IN this chapter *we have made prominent that side of human history which is generally unwritten.* In reading the history of by-gone times we obtain but a very superficial glance into the real life of the men who have figured therein. It is beyond the power of the historian to give us more. He can graphically depict the customs of the age, the fashionable dress of the court, and the commercial progress of the reign. Or he may portray the political creed of the statesman, the conquests of the warrior, the genius of the artist, and the true self-denial of the philanthropist. But further than this he cannot go; into the dim beyond he may not enter. The king stands as the centre of this wonderful record, and all minor personages are worthy of description in proportion as they circle near him. Thus the narrative frequently becomes one of jealousy and conflict; the men in authority one day are exiled from their country the next. These civil relationships can be written. But if a privileged author were permitted entrance to the soul-chamber of human history what facts unknown would be disclosed, what suspicions unwhispered would be confirmed, and how different would the printed narrative appear in comparison with that unpenned. However this cannot be.

The room of man's heart-life is locked; God holds the key, and but seldom lends it to the Christian, much less to the metaphysical analyst. Nor can we complain that the moral history of the dead is, to a certain extent, concealed from our view. We have not the ability to overlook the personality of others, and therefore must remain contented with the general aspect of their outward life. True, we can easily imagine that a disclosure of the world's inner history would be productive of good, yet it might also result in injury. Already the out-look upon human sin and woe is gloomy enough, and if the prospect were widened the terrible spectacle might lead us to despair. Certainly, there are two sides to this statement, for if the wickedness of national history were made known, its moral purity would also have to be unveiled. And although this would be the cause of joy to many, giving them to feel that there was much more true piety in the world than they had anticipated; it might also be the source of grief to others by making the conflict between good and evil appear more fierce, and inspiring them with fear as to the ultimate issue. However, that which is impossible to men is possible with God, hence what we do not find in human history we have in the Divine. In the Scriptures we are permitted occasional glimpses into the heart-life of individuals, and it is in them that we must gain our true knowledge of human nature. Here we learn that life does not consist in mere political or social externalisms, but in the deep conflict of the soul with evil. Thus, in the chapter before us, we are allowed to stand in the sanctuary of a Prophet's heart, and to hear his earnest devotions. We might call the following verses the biography of Jonah. Prayer is biography. If you wished to write the life of any man, the most effectual way to gain a knowledge of him would be to hear his secret petitions at the throne of grace. Then, considering himself alone with God, he would unfold the motive and method of his life as you had never seen them before. The biographical sketches of the present day would be much more beneficial if, instead of such extensive moralising, there were more prayers given, which may have been written by the deceased, in moments of devout reflection, during the most eventful periods of his life. Such a knowledge of the inner life of men, as revealed by prayer, is absolutely essential to true, unprejudiced biography. Even when listening to the public supplications of the sanctuary you may thereby obtain an insight into the moral life of those by whom they are offered. No man can rise in petition to heaven higher than the general fervour of his daily life. It is entirely impossible to counterfeit the richer influences of the Holy Spirit. Hence the pathos and unction of prayer, public or private, are true indexes to the worth of our manhood. Until now we have been almost inclined to look upon Jonah as an ordinary man, without much depth of character, but while listening to this prayer we discover in him a prophet-nature of the highest type. So there are multitudes with whom we associate in the ordinary performance of our daily avocation, they are considered by us as lacking in the sublime tendencies of life, but if we were to hear them pray, in the silence of their evening chamber, we should probably find that such was not the case. Thus, when we are inclined to place a low estimate upon the moral worth of our companions, who perhaps amid the rough contact of market life, may not exhibit all the loveliness of disposition we might wish, just think that there may be some hidden virtue underneath, which if revealed would touch their entire character into delightful harmony. Hence we must not judge according to appearance, but judge righteous judgment.*

Further, it will help us in the exposition of this chapter to remember *the very severe conflict which it discloses between the faith of Jonah and his circumstances.* Here he is living in the belly of the great fish, totally ignorant as to how long he will remain thus, and also as to the likelihood of an escape. There appears nothing to inspire hope within him, and this temporary safety may, after all, be a mere aggravation of his punishment. But while circumstances are adverse to the Prophet, there is within his heart a divine principle, which sustains him in fervent prayer. Thus the chapter stands as a relief and counterpart to the former, proving that the faith of Jonah was strong, and that disobedience was not to be taken as the normal condition of his life. Seldom have men anywhere been called to combat with circumstances more trying, and probably we may search the annals of history in vain for a more complete mastery over them. It would seem that while in this extremity, his soul gathered a moral fortitude appropriate to the hour. Let us then learn from this narrative, never to yield the supremacy of our moral character to the force of circumstances, however

---

*John 7:24.

powerful, or accidental they may be, but to resist them
by diligent prayer to God.

Then ˙Jonah prayed unto the Lord his God out of the fish's
belly.—*Verse* 1.

First we will consider *the fact here stated, namely,
that Jonah prayed while in the belly of the great fish.*
It was quite necessary, under the circumstances, that
this communication should be made. Because had we
not been so informed we could not have imagined that
such would have been the case. Upon finding his condition to be so perilous, *Jonah might have given way to
despair*, which would altogether have unfitted him for
supplication. How many times have we, when in difficulty, been so completely surprised, and overwhelmed
with grief, that all our spiritual energy has been para-
lyzed. Again, if he had not yielded to despair, *he might
have lapsed into an indifferent carelessness*, waiting
inactively for the pending issue, alternating between
hope and fear. Have we not felt, when in sorrow, that
all the powers of the soul have, unknown to us,
become silent, anxiously awaiting the indications of
future destiny. *Jonah might have given way to profanity*. Some men of degenerate life, placed in his
circumstances, would have vented their feelings in the
language of blasphemy, wishing that their wretched
existence might be annihilated rather than spared to
grapple with the mysterious future awaiting them.
But when Prophets are in trouble they do not generally
act like other men, their moral greatness only suffers a
momentary eclipse, and then shines forth in all the
heavenly effulgence of devoted piety.

We cannot but remark that *it required a continued discipline to bring Jonah to his knees*. The tempest had appealed to him, he had heard the cries of the mariners for help, and had himself been detected by a casting of the lot, yet we are not told by the narrative that he prayed. Even if he had responded to the command of the ship-master, in the previous chapter, his petitions must have been formal and fettered, he being surrounded by so many listeners, whose attention had lately been directed to him. But now, free from the restriction of an intruding presence, he pours out his soul before that God who alone could comfort and help him. The great object of all heavenly discipline is to produce this result. Some men are stubborn and will not yield to the holy influences of grief; others are independent and try to rise above the sorrowful events of life by the sheer force of their own nature. Happy they who, when running messengers announce the destruction of property, and the death of children, are like the devout Job who "fell down upon the ground and worshipped."*

Also, consider *to whom the prayer of Jonah was presented*. "Then Jonah prayed unto the Lord his God." The Prophet had too much knowledge, and felt too much contrition of heart, for the past disobedience, to pray to anyone else. Also he wanted release from his situation of peril, and he knew that to ask either angel or saint for it would be vain. Hence, he prays to the Being from whose presence he had endeavoured to flee. This picture is most true to life and history. Men forsake God, and when involved in trouble, they immediately apply to Him for help. How

---

*Job 1:20.

contradictory is our life; how opposite in its tendencies. Jonah prayed unto the Lord *his* God. As a Prophet he stood in most intimate relationship to the divine Being. He was linked to Jehovah by all the associations of the past, and by the dearest anticipations of the future, which even his present condition of woe could not remove from him. There was yet something within his heart that bound him to the Eternal.

Learn further from this narrative *that prayer is not dependent for its efficacy upon the place in which it is offered."* "Then Jonah prayed unto the Lord his God out of the fish's belly." What will our High Church friends say to this? There is no Ritualism here, no grand Cathedral, not even the ordinary convenience for worship, and yet from this rude temple there rises to heaven a most devout prayer. Stones do not make a Cathedral. The praying soul can make a hut into a church. Not that we would contend from this narrative that the house of prayer should be unbeautified; but, simply, that mere externalisms are not absolutely requisite to reverent homage. The devout man can worship anywhere; no matter how rude the structure into which he may have entered, there his soul can commune with heaven.

Again, we learn *that prayer can be offered under outward circumstances the most unfavourable.* As, in opposition to the Ritualist, prayer is not dependent for its value upon the place from which it is presented, so, for the encouragement of the honest Christian we assert that it can rise superior to external disadvantages. Jonah prayed in the belly of the great fish, while in the mighty waters. Surely we cannot imagine a more unfavourable condition for prayer than this. There was everything to divert his thought, and to disquiet his soul; but, notwithstanding, he holds intercourse with heaven. Will not this example of communion with God reprove many of us, who in circumstances much more congenial, have neglected it. How frequently do we hear men say, that they cannot worship God amidst the bustle of secular life. Is not the workshop as likely a place for prayer as a whale's belly? Are not the circumstances far more unfavourable in the latter case than in the former? If, then, Jonah could make known the want of his heart to God amid these difficulties, surely no working man, however severe his toil, or uncongenial the scenes of its performance, will make his surroundings an excuse for the neglect of devotion. True, we must regard the case of Jonah as somewhat exceptional, but we cannot put aside its teaching on that account; on the contrary, it becomes all the more forceful, enhancing our condemnation, in that while our religious experience may triumph over the accidental events of life, it so seldom does.

And said, I cried by reason of mine affliction unto the Lord, and he heard me; out of the belly of hell cried I, and thou heardest my voice.—*Verse* 2.

This verse teaches *the subduing influence of deep affliction*. It gives pathos to human life. The beauty of many characters would never have been brought out but for suffering. Grief intensifies all the nobler faculties of the soul until they become capable of the highest spiritual devotion. Men whose hearts have been hard-

ened by continued sunshine have been softened, and
fitted for the reception of holy truth, by the shower of
adversity. When individuals are placed in circumstances
of dire calamity, when all human aid is vain, then it is
that the soul is brought to prayer. At such times men
gather *earnestness.* Jonah "cried" unto the Lord.
There is nothing half-hearted about his prayer. It is
the natural outcome of a soul full of trouble. The
sailor may take things easily when the sky is bright,
when the waves ripple out their cheerful music; but
when the ship is reeling beneath the storm he must be
earnest. So if we are indifferent about the meaning of
life in happiness, we cannot be in sorrow, as then God
explains it to us, and we must either pray for mercy to
forgive the past, or await in suspense the ultimate
consequence of our folly.

This verse illustrates *the Divine sympathy with
human grief.* "And he heard me." How very touching is this prayer. Although Jonah had been disobedient to the Divine call, yet he was not entirely removed
from the sympathy of God. Do not these words touch
a cord within your hearts ? "And he heard me." Can
you not remember a similar incident in your own history ?
When great affliction was removed, or timely aid afforded,
and you uttered them in accents of joy ? Philosophers
talk about submitting prayer to a physical test. Christian men do not require any such a proof of its divinity ;
their own experience is sufficient. Here we have *Divine
condescension.* "And he heard *me.*" God harkened
to the supplication of Jonah, and sent him the deliverance he needed. Whose prayer was it that the Lord
heard ? It was not the cry of an unfallen saint, but of a

disobedient prophet. Surely here is condescension, and from it we may take encouragement, learning that God will hear the prayer of a penitent backslider. But here is also *Divine mercy*. In that Jonah was delivered from such a perilous and uncomfortable position. So the mercy of God is ever manifested towards men, in that he brings them forth from the circumstances in which their sins have placed them. "And he heard me." There beams out from this sentence a smile for the world. Oh that it may subdue our hearts into lowly gratitude.

Further, we learn from this verse *that the Divine help reaches to the deepest extremity of our grief.* "Out of the belly of hell I cried and thou heardest my voice." Our friends are generally willing to extend their aid in the trials of life, but only to a certain point,—if our sorrow travels beyond that, they leave us; and thus, when in the greatest need, we are often companionless. Not so with the Divine sympathy. It reaches to our deepest woe; penetrating even to the darkness and confinement of the grave; and when our friends are willing to compassionate our grief, it may be that they have not the ability to do so; hence, again, we are left to tread the dark ravine alone. But the power of Christ to remove sorrow, is equal to His sympathy with it; both are immeasurable. Never have circumstances been known to limit the outcome of His love, or to prevent the exercise of Divine help.

It is worthy of observation that *the prayer of Jonah was vocal.* "And thou heardest my *voice.*" Though the Prophet was in the belly of the great fish he yet retained the power of speech. He was not in a trance,

or in a passive state of helplessness. He lived, and all
the powers of his being were employed in supplication
to God. We might in this respect imitate the example
of Jonah. Vocal utterance is often a great help to
devotion. It stimulates thought and so prevents
lethargy. As we use the voice in our daily intercourse
with men, why should we not also, yea with far greater
propriety, in our communion with heaven. The power
of language was not merely given to us for our amuse-
ment or gratification, but also for the articulation of
religious feeling. Therefore, what more natural than
that it should be thus employed. But, while we suggest that our prayers might be spoken, we likewise
urge that the utmost discretion be used; in order to
avoid any thing like pretence or display.

For thou hadst cast me into the deep, in the midst of the seas;
and the floods compassed me about: all thy billows and thy waves
passed over me.—*Verse 3.*

No doubt many will be inclined to regard this as
figurative language, but we think that it is capable of
a literal interpretation. Are we not warranted in this
supposition by a reference to the previous chapter,
where it is recorded that Jonah was cast into the sea?
Thus the verse becomes much more natural and expressive in describing the actual rather than any imaginary
condition of the Prophet. We do not wish, however,
merely to contemplate it in its bearing towards Jonah,
but as typical of the discipline by which disobedient
Christians are visited.

We gather from this verse *that the discipline of God*

is frequently severe. " For thou hadst cast me into the
deep, in the midst of the seas; and the floods compassed me about." We must remember that the
Divine discipline is often penal. It was so in reference
to Jonah. It was designed to punish him for his neglect of the heavenly commission which required him to
go to Nineveh. Thus we must confess that he brought
this trouble upon himself. But this discipline was not
merely penal, but corrective, designed to bring back
Jonah to his Prophet-character and position; also to
impress more forcefully upon his mind the necessity of
obedience to any future commands that might be given.
Hence, this discipline had not merely reference to the
past of Jonah's life, but also to its future. God knew
that there were yet important commands awaiting, and
he therefore desires, by these circumstances of peril, so
to influence the moral disposition of the runaway Prophet that he may be willing to perform them. The
unacted drama of our lives is well known to God, thus
He can make the present trial, through which we may
be passing, fit us for, as yet, unknown emergencies.
Thus the Divine discipline, though it may be severe,
has a twofold aspect: first, of punishment for bye-gone
unfaithfulness; and secondly, of strengthening for the
future. We all know, probably, from deep experience,
that the discipline of God is often severe. We have
been cast into the deep, in the midst of the seas, and
the floods have compassed us about; but even, then we
have had, like the Prophet, the consolation of prayer,
and through that we have gained Divine help to our
final deliverance.

Again, we find from this verse *that Jonah looked*

*through the secondary causes, which had been the occasion
of his grief, to the Great First Cause.* " For *thou* hadst
cast me into the deep." There is no Atheism here,
but a holy recognition of God, in a most painful event
which had overtaken the Prophet. Jonah might have
attributed his circumstances of peril to *himself,* in that
he told the sailors to throw him overboard! Or, animated by the disposition which human nature generally
manifests, to make others responsible for its sorrow, he
might have attributed his position to the hard hearted-
ness of the *mariners* who had cast him into the deep.
But no. His own suggestion, and the conduct of the
crew in reference thereto, are entirely forgotten in his
abiding remembrance of that God against whom he
had sinned. And in this Jonah was perfectly right.
To have blamed himself would have been futile, and to
have reflected upon the treatment which he had received from the sailors, would not only have been cruel,
but unjust, as they had done everything in their power
to promote his safety.* The teaching contained in this
part of the verse now under consideration is capable of
earnest application to most Christian people in the
present day. We want more thoroughly to look through
all minor causes, which may have brought painful
events upon us, to God, who worketh through them.
But for Him they could not touch us at any
point. Very frequently when even Christian families
are bereaved they attribute the death of their loved
one to this cause or that. Perhaps to the neglect of
the dead, who, when alive did not provide for the
inclemency of the weather, but exposed himself to the

---

*Jonah 1:12.   Jonah 1:13

damp or the cold; or, it may be, that the doctor, who attended the deceased in his last illness, not thoroughly understanding the nature of the malady, may not have administered the medicine most calculated to have removed it. And the sorrowful relatives, resting upon these facts, become somewhat querulous, giving way to vain regrets, or unkind insinuations. They probably say, that, if such a precaution had been taken, or such a medicine given, their lost one might have been even now living. Of course, we admit that all the discoveries of science and medicine should be used, and all care taken in such cases, but after this is done the result must be left with God; and if the issue is fatal, the medical attendant must be forgotten, and the darkness of surrounding circumstances dispelled by the brightness of a Divine Presence standing within the circle of our lives. "Thou hadst cast me into the deep."

Further, we learn from this verse *the benefit of a true knowledge of Scripture in times of severe moral discipline.* "All thy billows and thy waves passed over me." Jonah throughout this prayer shows a personal acquaintance with the Psalms current in his day. If you compare the second verse of this chapter with the sixth of the eighteenth Psalm, you will find even a verbal similarity, and in the verse now under review there is an unmistakable reference to the figurative language of the Psalmist, "Deep calleth unto deep at the noise of thy waterspouts: all thy waves and thy billows are gone over me."* However, we need not dwell longer upon the similarities of language used by Jonah in his prayer, and that frequently employed by

*Psalm 42:7.

the Psalmist; a mere passing reference to the places in
which they may be found will suffice.* Thus we see
how thoroughly the mind of Jonah was saturated with
Divine truth.

We cannot but think that *this verbal acquaintance
with Scripture was a great aid to him in prayer.* It is
a grand thing to be able to pray Scripture. To be so
intimate with the inspired record that, when we come
to God in prayer, we can speak to Him in His
own language. We are aware that many regard
such a verbal knowledge of God's word as slavish and
unmeaning. And if the words are not accompanied
with the spirit of their instruction, this is true; but
when both are united, then may our knowledge of Holy
Writ be designated complete. There are times in
prayer when memory is more ready than utterance.
Also there are times when emotion is too deep for
expression in the scanty words of a human vocabulary.
Then the memory can lay hold of the words of God,
and by them the heart can utter its petition.

Then not only was the knowledge of Scripture a
great aid to Jonah in prayer, *but it was also a sublime
comfort to him in trouble.* Very likely the Prophet
would gather hope from the wonderful history of the
Psalmist, whose language he quoted. Jonah would
regard the continued deliverances of David as the
bright pledge of his own in due time. Scripture biography and truth always have a soothing effect upon
the grief-stricken spirit, giving it to feel that, as others
have, so it may, by Divine grace, emerge from its darkness with new moral beauty. Also the promises of
Holy Writ are encouraging, and frequently impart new

---

*Psalm 18:6; 30:3; 5:7.

strength into long tried, and almost fainting hearts.

But we come to the question, *How did Jonah acquire this knowledge of God's Word?* Was it the result of pious education at home, conducted with the assiduity and tenderness of a loving mother? Probably not. Was it consequent upon a long period of training prior to entering upon the duties of the Prophetic office? We cannot tell. Very likely it was the result of a long and continued attendance upon the Temple service. Amid all its worship there was nothing that had made so indelible an impression upon his mind as the singing of those primitive, but deeply pathetic, Psalms. Their music had often thrilled his soul. But now that he is in trouble a remembrance of them returns to him more powerfully than ever, and they become the medium of communion with God. So should the service of our Christian Temples attract our attention, and inspire with interest, that all their ritual and teaching, may be indicative of themes for prayer. There are ideas gathered in the Sanctuary which can be suggested no where else, and it should be our great object to bring reflective minds, especially youthful, under their influence, that they may be fortified thereby for the emergencies of life.

" Then I said, I am cast out of thy sight; yet I will look again toward thy holy temple.—*Ver.* 4.

Here we have manifested *the alternate impulses of the human soul.* Jonah, in the first part of this verse, says that he is cast out from the presence of the Lord ; and in the second, that he will look again toward the holy temple, indicating that despair and hope were

alternating within him.   The sentiments of our nature
are sometimes as changing as the evening play of light
and shade upon the mountain side.

*This alternation of feeling is common to people in
trouble.* Bereavement saddens, but the Comforter gives
joy; poverty threatens, but Divinely commissioned
ravens prevent want; life appears to close in with
darkest shadows, but at eventide there is light.   And
thus the experiences of grief, when touched by the
Divine finger, are turned into instruments of praise.
It is this association of God with our lives that pro-
duces the impulse of joy, and but for it our existence
would be a weird monotony of grief.

*This alternation of feeling is common to people in
prayer.* It would appear that while Jonah was praying
he felt more than before the deep meaning of his
punishment; hence his despondency.   But being led
by devotion from his circumstances of peril, to a Diviner
presence near, he appears more tranquil in anticipation
of the future.   No one can tell the varied emotions that
ebb and flow through a penitent heart, when pleading
for the pardon of past unfaithfulness.   At such times
new forces seem to enter, and keep the soul in continued unrest.   Therefore, when in this condition of
alternate gloom and doubt, do not yield to the former
but regard the conflict as the condition and pledge of
a higher life, soon to dawn upon the suppliant nature.

Even *the highest Christian life is subject to this alternation of feeling.* As we behold a great diversity in
the appearance of the outer world, so in the world of
the purest soul there is constant change.   Monotony
of feeling is unknown in heaven; there with untiring

capacity, and holy ability, the brightest spirits are ever entering into new experiences of truth and love. And for saints on earth never to experience a lofty emotion, never for the peaceful surface of their heart-life to be broken by the sweep of some great impulse dashing onward to the infinite, would be to degrade their manhood. Progress is the chief element of the joy of heaven. And if our life was never moved by its effort, our happiness would be meteoric, brilliant for a moment, and then going out for ever. We all know that advancement of any kind means conflict and occasional depression; now the soul is lit up with the Divine fire of hope; again the flames are extinguished, and the smouldering embers only cause a denser darkness to come over it. But owing to the weakness of faith in Christ, the calm of our daily life is more frequently interrupted by evil than progress.

Unholy men sometimes say that they cannot understand the moral fluctuation of the Christian life, that it is contrary to their experience, as they are never subject to it. They urge that the calm of their lives is but seldom interrupted; and relatively this may be true of many, they live in ignorance of an ever-nearing peril, their eyes are closed and they see not the yawning precipice toward which they are steadily walking. But of others it is not true, their natures are the abode of impulses far darker and fiercer than any that ever dwelt within a Christian heart—impulses that are never succeeded by joy, but only by a yet more terrible passion, prophetic of a future, where all the now latent powers of the soul will be awakened into a terror which nothing will be able to subdue.

Further, we gather from this verse *that the realization of sinful desire is its own punishment.* We read in the former chapter that "Jonah rose up to flee unto Tarshish *from the presence of the Lord.*" * Now he complains that he is cast out from the Divine sight. Thus showing that the attainment of a wicked project is its own penalty. All sin is a fleeing from God, and will be sure to meet with solemn retribution. Frequently men go in the pursuit of extravagant and unlawful pleasure, and directly they grasp the pleasing phantom which has so long enticed their thought, and which looked so lovely in the distance, they find that it is a demon surrounded by a multitude whose ruin may be regarded as prophetic. How often have we heard of men murdering their relatives in the hope of gain. The deed was done. The money was obtained. But, alas! where is the joy anticipated? Are they not enshrined with a mantle of darkness, from which they find it impossible to escape? Even though detection come not yet, a sad remembrance of the tragedy will never leave them, and conscience, like a flame of fire, will light up their inmost soul to unfold yet more forcefully its horrid meaning. Thus we see the inseparable connection between sin and retribution; one following on the same line as the other, and almost with equal step. In this we must recognize a wise arrangement of the Divine government, for the prevention of that which so much mars the beauty of character, and destroys the happiness of life.

Lastly, we learn from this verse, *that banishment from the presence of God is the penal element in trouble.*

---

*Jonah 1:3

" I am cast out of thy sight." Here is true retribution, and almost more than the human soul can bear. When in grief men do not so much look at the physical pain they endure, but at its mysterious association with Divine providence, and it is this that causes their alarm. To be cast out from the sight of God, which is the moral side of discipline, is to be cut off from the fontal source of all happiness—to be without protection in danger, comfort in sorrow, guidance in difficulty, and hope in future destiny. The Divine presence is the sun of our moral life, guilding with hope, filling with cheerful influences ; its absence makes our night, wherein the destroying angel visits, and breathes death upon our first-born.

The waters compassed me about, even to the soul : the depth closed me round about, the weeds were wrapped about my head.— *Verse* 5.

This verse teaches *the literalness of human suffering.* We frequently hear men talk about suffering as though it were something majestic and sublime. Books very often depict it in this light. In the memorials of good people, who have departed this life, the pain they endured is so described as almost to render it poetic. We hear so much about the beneficial effect of sorrow upon moral character, that, beholding it at a distance, sketched in such lovely colors, we are in danger of forgetting its deep underlying meaning. The sufferer himself does not regard it through these charmed media, but feels that "the waters compass him about, and that the weeds are wrapped about his head." So true is it that the sorrow of life is not imaginary or unreal, but literal, and often severely so.

Again, we see in this verse *the surrounding power of deep affliction*. "The waters compassed me about, even to the soul : the depth closed me round about." For how many chapters in your past history would this be an appropriate heading ? If we could but read the lives of many thronging our sanctuaries and walking our streets, how fitly would they be described, in a moral sense, by this language of the Prophet ? There are times when trouble does not merely touch us at a given point, but envelopes our entire being. Every faculty of the soul is brought under its pathetic influence. In fact, as an island is surrounded by the sea, so our hearts are often encompassed with grief, whose mighty billows dash upon them with relentless fury.

We also see illustrated in this verse *the confusing power of deep affliction*. "The weeds were wrapped about my head." Sorrow is *intellectually* confusing. The weeds were wrapped about Jonah's *head*. Then it sometimes happens that the intelligent powers of the soul are so completely overwhelmed that they cannot command the power of consecutive thought, and therefore are not to be relied upon for direction. Sorrow is often *morally* confusing. All the feelings of the heart are intensified, they become nervous, and therefore tremblingly undertake any means for its removal. At such times God is the only efficient guide of the soul, for if men confide in their own reason, or impulse, they are sure to become the more entangled in weeds.

I went down to the bottoms of the mountains ; the earth with
her bars was about me for ever: yet hast thou brought up my life
from corruption, O Lord, my God.—*Verse* 6.

There can be no doubt but that this verse *describes
the circumstances of Jonah as they really appeared to
him.* Of course, at such a time he would not be in a
very calm state for reflection, and it is not unlikely that
he may have received a distorted impression of things
around him. But, even after making due allowance for
this, we cannot but feel that the picture contained in
this verse is most graphic. It is most expressive. The
remembrance of that time would probably never leave
the Prophet : its strange experiences were engraven
upon his heart. And being thus supremely interested
in the unprecedented drama, he pictures it to our view,
in all the minuteness of vivid recollection.

Here we have *the misery of Jonah presented under
the aspect of an imprisonment.* " I went down to the
bottoms of the mountains ; the earth with her bars was
about me for ever." Viewed in this light, *the imprisonment of Jonah was somewhat novel.* Frequently had
individuals been punished for disobedience to the commands of God, but never before in such a manner.
And certainly never since has the watery deep been
turned into a dungeon for a runaway Prophet. The
retributions of human life are frequently novel. They
are not always after the old patterns. Sometimes they
move on an unusal line. Hence, men can never tell
what will be the exact result of their sin, which should
be an additional motive to refrain from it. *Jonah
was companionless in this imprisonment.* There was

no enemy near to taunt the Prophet with unfaithfulness. Neither was their a friend near him to utter words of comfort and hope. He was entirely alone. In fact, his was the only cell in the prison. No human being could have reached him even had they known him to be alive, or were acquainted with his whereabouts, much less have rendered any assistance. Sin always places men in positions of solitude, either through the unheard of circumstances into which it may have brought them, or through the disgust of better-minded folk; and some men's lives are so vile that loneliness is the only method to insure reflection, and to prevent their evil designs upon society.

We gather from this verse *that Jonah was brought out from his imprisonment.* "Yet hast thou brought up my life from corruption, O Lord my God." This deliverance was, humanly speaking, most *unlikely.* Jonah was regarded by all as a lost man. What could secure his restoration? Surely, nothing. Had he not been brought into his present circumstances by sin, and who will imagine that mercy could be associated with so strange a punishment. This deliverance was *highly benevolent.* "Thou hast brought up my *life* from corruption." What will not a man give for his life? It was a treasure beyond all price that was restored to the Prophet. This deliverance was *Divinely wrought.* "Yet hast *thou* brought up my life from corruption." No one else could have given freedom to the Prophet. God's thoughts are not as our thoughts, hence when we consider men beyond the reach of mercy, there often comes to them an angel which opens noiselessly the great prison door in which they are, and striking their

fetters to the ground, bids them follow him to freedom.
It is better to fall into the hands of God than of man.
This deliverance was *recognized and appreciated by
Jonah*. " O Lord, my God." These words are full of
meaning. They at once express the faith and joy of
the Prophet. All the old feelings of his former life
came into his heart again, and he was determined that
future obedience should prove his gratitude for the
timely interposition.

Finally, we see in this verse *how thoroughly God can
adapt the existing state of material nature to human
conduct*. Frequently are men heard to say that God
cannot punish the wicked in Hell, as no such place can
be found in the arrangements of material nature.
Even if we admit this, what advantage do our objectors
gain? Do we not find from the temporary confinement
of Jonah within the sea, that without the slightest
alteration in nature, God can make the existing
condition of things accomplish His will. True, the
objects around us assume certain shapes, and are
designed for a certain purpose, but for us to say that
they can be put to no other, is simply to assert our
ignorance. Even the man who has made the furthest
research, and who knows most about the working of
material nature, is supremely ignorant of the unknown
possibilities of which it may be capable. It is very
much like a transformation scene. As out of the same
canvas there appears to come a new picture fitted for
the changed condition of the drama ; so at the bidding
of God the present appearances of nature could be
immediately adapted to another condition of life. The
natural world is under the perfect control of the Divine

Being, and surely, therefore, he will not be at a loss to accomplish his purpose by it. For all we know, even now there may be in some hidden spot, a place reserved for the finally impenitent, but if there is not, God could commission a great fish to become a hell.

When my soul fainted within me I remembered the Lord : and my prayer came in unto thee, into thine holy temple.—*Verse 7*.

We learn from this verse *that a remembrance of God is the only refuge of a troubled soul.* "When my soul fainted within me I remembered the Lord." Here the Prophet indicates that till now he had forgotten the Divine Being, and this is in harmony with the narrative which we have contemplated. For certainly if such had not been the case he would not have persisted in flight as he did. This forgetfulness contains the secret of Jonah's peril. For when men, especially Christian men, are guilty of it they are sure to come to grief ; from that very moment a dark shadow comes upon the pathway of their soul which no joy can charm away, and the meaning of which only eternity will reveal. Hence we cannot but gather from this history that forgetfulness of God is *foolish*, being the germ of all trouble ; *criminal*, being the true explanation of all punishment ; and *unjustifiable*, being entirely inexcusable. Very frequently are men in difficulty *through their own misdoing*, and when the moral fortitude of their soul is exhausted, they remember God, and obtain rest in His mercy. But there are afflictions which come upon the godly man from another cause, not from *poverty or bereavement*, but from the apparent discrepancy of past history, and *the seeming confusion of moral character in the world at present.* He sees that piety is down-trodden, and that vice is triumphant in many instances. Being at a loss to find the solution of this dark problem, he is tempted to complain of the unequal conflict of life, forgetting that God has higher rewards for His people than merely temporal. A sensitive heart, troubled by this out-look upon human society, can only find comfort by the remembrance of God. He is equitable in character, and parental in regard for pure souls; hence we may rest assured that the present can and will be explained on some principle as yet unknown to us, and that the future, which is far more important, will no doubt open up this mystery of apparent confusion.

Again we learn from this verse *that a remembrance of God has an invigorating and devotional effect upon the soul.* "When my soul fainted within me I remembered the Lord: and my prayer came in unto thee, into thine holy temple." Thus the remembrance of God prompted Jonah to deep thought and earnest prayer. If we were to retain an habitual recollection of God our life would be one continued act of devotion. It would impart to our conduct a beauty unsurpassed, which men would have to recognize as Divine. It would comfort in sorrow, strengthen in temptation, prompt to duty, and invest life with a dignity beyond comparison. Our homes and shops would no longer be the scenes for the manifestation of strife and fraud, but for the outbeaming of a Divine Presence resident within us. Do you ask how we are to remember God? We reply by urging not merely a mental contemplation of the perfection of His character, not merely a casual reading of historical revelations which He has made of Himself, but by a living heart-faith in His abiding mercy.

Lastly, *we will call your attention to Jonah's designation of the Temple.* " Into thine holy temple." " The prayer of the Prophet came to God in his temple, which is not to be intended as taken of the heaven, the chief seat of His majesty and residence of His power, (although in general all the prayers of His elect and chosen do ascend and go up thither), but in more special manner it is meant of the Temple which Solomon erected, where, together with the ark of the covenant, and the cherubims, and the mercy-seat, the presence of God's grace was in most peculiar sort. And this house was to the Jews a visible sign and sacrament thereof; so that, according to the request which Solomon made to God, they repaired thither when anything did oppress them, as appeareth by Hezekiah, who laid open the letter of Sennacherib in the Temple before the Lord.* Yea, whensoever the Israelites were in a strange land, in bondage,† and called upon the Lord earnestly, they did turn themselves to that coast which way this house did stand." ‡

Jonah regarded the Temple as belonging to God, and therefore as holy. We ought, as Christian people, to hold our Sanctuaries in the highest reverence, ever associating with them all that is connected with prayer and God. They are holy because consecrated to the purposes of our higher and devotional life, and also because of the very choice and happy memories, with

---

*1 Kings 8:31-33; Isaiah 37:14.   †Daniel 6:10.
‡Archbishop Abbot on Jonah, vol. 1, page 302.

which the past of our history has invested them.
Therefore, whether we are distant from, or are even
participating in the service of the church, let the words
of Jonah be always on our lips and in our hearts—
"thine holy temple."

They that observe lying vanities forsake their own mercy.—
Verse 8.

In this verse *Jonah is giving us the result of his own
bitter experience."* "They that observe lying vanities
forsake their own mercy." Never before the last few
days had this truth been more forcefully brought before
the attention of the Prophet, it had occupied his mind
in thoughtful intervals, and had often been on his lips
as a preacher, but now it is ingrained into his very
being, by a phenomenon that cannot be forgotten.
Experience is generally an effective teacher, and such
men as Jonah are seldom unmindful of her instruction.
True, she is sometimes harsh in her method of tuition,
as he had just proved, but her ultimate design is good.
There are no doubt many present who have been made
to feel the significance of this verse. It may be there
are others who have yet to learn that its utterance is
correct, if so, permit the distant vision of a Prophet's
misery to teach, rather than dire calamity which will
inevitably arrest the wanderings of a wicked life.

We have in this verse *a course of conduct indicated.*
"They that observe lying vanities."* Life with many
is vanity and falsehood, there being nothing substantial

---

*"They that observe lying vanities, i.e.(by the force of the Hebrew
form) that diligently watch, pay deference to, court, sue, vanities of
vanities, vain things, which prove themselves vain at last, failing the
hopes which trust in them." — Pusey on *Minor Prophets*.

or real about it. Men are living in a vain show, and
are spell-bound by a dream. But this cannot be the
case long, as the charm of such a delusion will have to
be broken, either by the numerous voices which now
speak of another world, or by the awful realities of that
world breaking forth upon the careless soul, even while
in the noontide of its pleasure and hope. Who, then,
are the individuals mentioned in this verse, and what
are the vanities they pursue ? *All who make money the
chief good of life.* Those who make wealth the great
object after which they strive, and in the effort expend
all the enthusiasm of their nature—who even when it
is gained do not use it for barter, enhancing the
good of society, but hoard it up in secret places to
gratify, by an occasional thought, its covetous owner.
Or, it may be, that, far from this, the successful merchant gathers money, and then spends it in reckless
luxury and wanton debauchery. In either case, whether
wealth is desire in itself, or for the luxury it commands,
—it is a falsehood, and will one day laugh in defiant
mockery upon all who have observed it.

They observe lying vanities *whose great desire is for
fame and social distinction.* We find this abundantly
proven by a reference to the history of the past.
There we find that many, renowned for exploit and
genius, being elevated to positions of national honor,
have either experienced untimely disgrace, or spent
their lives in the deepest unrest. A man whose highest
aspiration is after fame may grasp the meteor, but very
likely it will scathe the hand that tries to appropriate it.
To put confidence in the uncertain favour of those
around is to observe lying vanities.

They observe lying vanities *who live without a truly practical and constant recognition of God.* For a time Jonah had removed his life from the guardian care of God to direct it himself. Prior to this the Divine will had been his guide, but now circumstances have arisen contrary to his expectation and wish; hence he has determined to become his own pilot. And with the awful issue, of even this temporary rejection of God, we are all well acquainted. Hence we find that to neglect the revelations of the Divine Will, or the indication of Providence, or in fact to live, even casually, without a devout recognition of God, is to forsake our own mercy. From the very day that the Prophet had taken ship for Tarshish, his life had been one long continuation of difficulty and trouble. So we need not plunge into the absurdities of Atheism to commit sin ; a momentary forgetfulness of God may involve us in grief, and cover us with sorrow of even three days duration. " Some trust in chariots, and some in horses : but we will remember the name of the Lord our God." *

They observe lying vanities *who embrace false systems of religion.* Roman Catholicism is a lying vanity, investing a certain class of men called priests with almost the attributes of God. We fear that this system is a falsehood, the wickedness of which only eternity will reveal to many deluded by it. *Ritualism* is a lying vanity, trying to make men think that true piety consists in external show, and in the performance of the body rather than in the emotions of the soul. *Unitarianism*—a religion without a true Christ, a Christ who can respond to the yearnings of the human heart—is a

---

*Psalm 20:7.

lying vanity which removes the dearest hope of our life, and makes the future one of despair. Other dogmas there are of a like tendency, and equally fatal in their result, such as relate to the supreme efficacy of works unbeautified by the hidden but essential power of faith. These falsehoods can neither feed the soul nor calm its disquiet. The eternal truth of God, immutable as its Author, revealed to the world in Jesus Christ, is the only trustworthy inspiration and hope of an immortal spirit; and to reject it is to forsake our own mercy.

This verse indicates *that this course of conduct is often pursued with great eagerness.* They diligently watch lying vanities. We cannot enter the scene of merchandise, read the record of public doings, or visit the churches of our land, without being convinced that men most earnestly pursue lying vanities. *This course of conduct is also degrading.* They that follow it serve lying vanities. Is it not so? For men, endowed with immortality, with aspiration that can reach to God, and with thought that can dwell in Heaven, to narrow their heart and mind to the limit of this world, is to subordinate their sympathies to momentary concerns, and to lower their manhood by a worship of the created. Truly, this is degradation of which only moral human life could be capable. *This course of conduct is wilful.* "Forsake their own mercy." After every motive has been urged, like examples of obstinate folly adduced; in full knowledge of the probable consequence, they wantonly leave the true and observe the false. *The ultimate destiny of this conduct is self-destruction.* They forsake the mercy which they ought to have naturally for themselves.; the kindly sympathy which others would extend to them, and also the Divine compassion, which is the brightest charm of life. And thus they ensconce themselves in their own mad folly; shut in so that no ray of pity can touch them at any point. And what is this but moral suicide of which only the truest insanity would be guilty. Lamentably they forsake their own mercy.

But I will sacrifice unto thee with the voice of thanksgiving; I will pay that that I have vowed. Salvation is of the Lord.— *Verse* 9.

In this verse we have set forth *the nature of true gratitude.* Very probably some new feature of hope had presented itself to the imprisoned Prophet, or some devout impulse may have taken possession of his soul—hence the language of the verse. *The gratitude of Jonah was sincere.* There was no pretence about it. The circumstances in which he had been placed during the last few days had rendered him intensely solemn. He felt that his continued life was attributed to the kindly interposition of God, and that therefore the deepest gratitude was due to Him. *The gratitude of Jonah was devout.* "I will sacrifice unto thee." It was no trifling expression of sentiment. It was not regarded as a necessary component of his prayer, but it was the unstudied outcome of his soul. He felt that he was in personal contact with God, and therefore his gratitude was reverent and humble. *The gratitude of Jonah was unconcealed.* "I will sacrifice unto thee with the *voice* of thanksgiving." He was not afraid to acknowledge his indebtedness to God before others; his disobedience had been open, and was it not therefore due to the Divine mercy that his deliverance should be equally well known. The same courage that prompted him to the former would, when sanctified by prayer, lead to the latter. A true soul cannot be voiceless about the love of God.

The gratitude of Jonah was practical. "I will pay that that I have vowed." He did not forget the past in the joy of the present, nor was his first impulse to enter upon the happiness of deliverance before the duty of it. He was careful not merely to recognize the promise made in his grief, but also to work it out to the very best of his ability. How many of us while listening to these words are reminded of instances in which we have broken many a solemn vow made in affliction. We have not gone forth with the spiritual influence derived from sorrow to do that which we had promised. And even to-day our vows are unheeded!

Further, we have in this verse *the highest acknowledgement of true gratitude.* "Salvation is of the Lord." This was the highest note of gratitude that the Prophet could reach. He appears to have been somewhat at a loss for thought and language, whereby to extol the goodness of God, hence he breaks out in this exhaustive expression which is a miniature Bible.

Review for a moment *the nature of this salvation.* It does not merely refer to that which we all realize upon a personal trust in Christ, but to all those kindly deliverances which are so welcome to men in peril. *The author of this salvation.* "Salvation is of the Lord." It is not by the exercise of reason, or forethought, that we are removed from the unhappy circumstances of life, but by the considerate providence of God. Hence we ought to blend our thanksgiving with that of the Prophet saying—"Salvation is of the Lord."

And the Lord spake unto the fish, and it vomited out Jonah upon the dry land.—*Verse* 10.

The subject of this verse *is a Prophet's rescue.* Now the end of all has come, the discipline and discomfort of the last few days are over, and the once disobedient, but now restored Prophet, is allowed to reenter upon the great mission of his life. *This rescue was welcome.* Who can imagine the feelings of Jonah when first he stood upon dry land again. Surely he would be unable to analyze them. Truly wonder and joy would be the most prominent impulses of his soul. He would survey the landscape, with its tint and shade, so welcome to his eye. No longer confined within the dungeon of the waters, he would be free to wander wherever he liked. No change in circumstances could have been more welcome or surprising to him. *The rescue was complete.* Jonah was vomited out upon " *dry land.*" He was not cast out upon the waters, still to be in a condition of peril until picked up by a passing ship. No ; his deliverance was perfect, and wrought in a manner most likely to enhance his final comfort. Upon what shore he was cast, and how he fared thereon we are not told. *This rescue was instructive.* Both to the Prophet and ourselves. It would teach him never to forsake God again if he wanted his life to be peaceful and happy. It would give him to feel that a second act of disobedience might not end so well, and, therefore, we may suppose that a holy fear of grieving God would dwell within him. Such are the lessons we may gather from the narrative.

This rescue was Divine in its method of accomplishment. "And the Lord spake unto the fish." In what manner God communicated with the fish we cannot say, but to indicate that there was intercourse of some kind, we are told that speech was employed. God spake and the world sprang into being; truly, then, He would not be at a loss to denote his will to the great fish. This language is accommodated to our ideas of human intercourse. *This rescue was easily accomplished.* "The Lord *spake* unto the fish." Only a word was spoken, and the Prophet was released from his dungeon.

Hence we cannot but learn *the entire control of God over the animal creation.* The fish was subject to His will. So were the lions in the case of Daniel. So was the snake which clung to the hand of the Apostle Paul. The brute world is under a Divine control, which has often been exerted for the safety and welfare of the good. We can hardly help feeling a sort of veneration for this fish which has preserved to us a Prophet, and all the hallowed instruction which we cannot but gather from a true contemplation of his prayer. This chapter is most valuable, and should be presented to the view of every penitent sinner, as the scarlet thread of his deliverance.

And so we finish our contemplation of one of the most instructive and pathetic chapters to be found in the whole round of history, secular or sacred. It contains indeed a true revelation of the soul's inner life. It shows the beneficent effect of trouble upon a prayerful heart; and, also, the nearness, the willingness, and the ability of God to aid imperiled human life. We regard the prayer of this chapter as a model for all Christian people. It is natural, specific, orderly, pathetic, and devout. Such a prayer cannot but attract the Divine attention. Altogether we look upon this chapter as being one of the greatest educational forces of our spiritual life. No sensitive man can read it without feeling that God speaks through its verses to his deepest nature.

> Father of everlasting grace,
> Be mindful of Thy changeless word;
> We worship toward that Holy Place,
> In which Thou dost Thy name record,
> Dost make Thy gracious nature known,
> That living Temple of Thy Son.

JONAH 3

WE are now about to enter upon the second part of Jonah's wonderful history. The narrative has so grown upon us in interest that we feel it impossible to withdraw ourselves from its charm. Our curiosity is aroused. We are anxious to know what became of Jonah after his return to "dry land." Did he at once set out for the Temple at Jerusalem, or for his home at Gath-helper? If so, with whom did he meet on the journey? Did he resume the Prophetic office, or the trade of his youth? Here the record is silent. But soon the silence is broken by a Divine voice, uttering again, to Jonah, the command of the first chapter. We listen. We wait in suspense, and almost involuntarily ask ourselves, " Will he obey ? " And right glad are we to find him shortly after, leaving home to enter upon the work he had so lately refused to undertake. Now there is an addition to the picture. The mariners of the first chapter have passed into oblivion, and Jonah is surrounded by a vast nation whose moral character will soon be changed from darkness into light. As though the great purpose of the narrative was to shew forth the abundant mercy of God toward individual and collective life, the same forgiveness was extended to a penitent nation as to a praying Prophet.

But the word of the Lord came unto Jonah the second time, saying.—*Verse* 1.

We should very much like to know when and where this message found Jonah ; whether he was at home in the house, or abroad in the field ?   Whether he was praying in the sanctuary, or working for his daily bread ?   It is, however, impossible to picture to our minds these minor details of the narrative, and there is little need that we should try, as sufficient is outlined to excite our interest and instruct our souls.

We observe that *this message came, nominally, to the same man as the first.*   " But the word of the Lord came unto *Jonah.*"   We say nominally because virtually it did not.   And this is very evident when we contrast the manner in which the two communications were treated.   The first was despised, whereas the second is accepted with true respect.   Surely, then, we are not in companionship with the same individual in both instances.   True, anyone looking at the Prophet now would say that his features were unaltered, that he was indeed the son of Amittai, born at Gath-helper. But manhood does not consist in mere external appearance, behind the face there is an immortal something called soul wherein consists true being.   Now the disposition of Jonah has changed in its attitude toward God, hence the new and advanced spiritual manhood, which we all so heartily admire.   Yes, we cannot but make a distinction between the Jonah of the first chapter, dark and moody, and that of the third, bright and obedient.   Let us then forget the past and give him that welcome to our esteem which his new conduct demands.

The most prominent lesson taught us in this verse is that *God gives to men successive opportunities for the accomplishment of their life-work.* " But the word of the Lord came unto Jonah the *second* time." We are not crushed by the weight of our first sin or failure. If we were few could have any thing like hope of the future. Life would become a dreary foreboding, lest any message committed to our care should be neglected, and entail final condemnation. The world would be full of wretched mortals upon whom there would rest the irrevocable woe of an unfulfilled mission. But such is not the case, as the voice of God speaks a second time to the erring Prophet, wishing him to go to Nineveh that he may yet retrieve the past and make the future glad.

This method of procedure is eminently Divine. When once we have abused, either intentionally or through ignorance, the confidence of our fellows they are not willing to trust us. They mark us either as untruthful or imbecile, and so do not seek again our aid in the plans of life. True, all do not act like this. Many, of sympathetic nature, are only too willing to give an unsuccessful brother a helping hand, in order that, perchance, his second attempt may be more happy than the first. But, after all, the generosity of these noble spirits is exceptional, and may, perhaps, loose its charm through airs of dignity ; while the forbearance of God is constant as it is considerate.

This method of treatment is eminently in harmony with the spirit of the Christian dispensation. True, as yet the Cross of Christ had not shone upon humanity in all its glory. Its blessing had not fully encircled mankind with all that was intended by a kindly Providence. Nevertheless, Christ being slain, in the foreknowledge of God, from the foundation of the world, the love of the Cross had already dawned upon the race. And in the early promise of the future, Jonah participated to the joy of his inner life. Under the law there could have been no second attempt to do the right. One offence would have involved eternal ruin. What a terrible thought! But we are not under the law, but under grace, which has come through Jesus Christ."* And in a dispensation so full of God, so radiant with compassion for the weak, what could be more consistent, or beautiful, than the hope it gives to the unfaithful that their ingratitude may be pardoned, and that a second trial may yet find them ready for the mission they once rejected.

Lastly, we find that *this method of Divine treatment is not interrupted by the basest ingratitude on the part of man.* This will be evident to all candid readers of Jonah's history. His ingratitude was indeed base. And that God regarded it as such is proved by the punishment he permitted to come upon it. Surely, then, here is a token of hope, not merely for the man of trivial offence, but also for anyone guilty of the most grievous wrong. Therefore, no backslider need turn away in despair, for here is a light to cheer him to the Cross, where a second time the great commission of his life may be renewed.

Arise, go to Nineveh, that great city, and preach unto it the preaching that I bid thee.—*Verse 2.*

*John 1:17.

We must regard this second message as somewhat different from the first. In the first chapter it was a command, but now it partakes more of the nature of a *test*. Its design is to ascertain the effect of the late discipline through which Jonah had passed ; to disclose the worth of his repentance, the meaning of his prayer, and the strength of his vows. Hence the Prophet's ready obedience to this second call proves his past sorrow to have been real, and his new manhood to be true.

But, notwithstanding this distinction, *the messages are the same in their ultimate requirement.* " Arise, go unto Nineveh." The same duty is enjoined as before. He must go to the same city and preach unto it. Divine claims are not nullified by disobedience, or altered to suit the caprice of individuals. They are unalterable, *because God is immutable.* He changeth not in his character, nor yet in the principle of his dealing with the race. He assigns to each a life mission, and ever requires that it should be faithfully attended to. *Also, because duty is imperative.* Never does God allow the message to go down to the moral character of the men ; on the contrary, the habit and thought of the man have to be lifted up to a level with the message, that it may be earnestly carried out.

Thus we find from this verse that *the true preacher has often to pass through severe discipline to prepare him for his work.* Men cannot be trained for the pulpit by unclouded happiness, by unbroken prosperity. Sorrow and peril impart to the preacher the most beautiful and effective elements of his character. They render him pathetic, capable of sympathy, which is so welcome to the down trodden and oppressed. This severe discipline also makes the preacher morally strong, able to overcome self, to enter upon arduous labour, and to contend courageously with antagonistic powers. Scientific instruction is useful to the minister of Divine truth, and a University training may be advantageous, but, after all, real pulpit power is only gained by the bitter experiences of life, and by contact with the stern realities of duty.

Further, we gather from this verse that *the true preacher must be Divinely commissioned.* "Arise, and go to Nineveh." Even after he may have been disciplined for the work of a minister, he must remain at home until he hears the voice of God saying, "Arise, go unto Nineveh." Any man undertaking such a work without a Divine warrant manifests a presumption that is sure to imperil his future safety and welfare. He may imagine that he has good qualifications for the work at Nineveh, but he has no right to go unless God sends him. The work is so important that it requires a special commission and discipline to prepare for it.

Again we learn from this verse that *the true preacher must declare the message of God.* "And preach unto it the preaching that I bid thee." From this it is very evident that a minister, Divinely commissioned, cannot preach what he likes. Even the theme of his discourse must be Divinely given, else it will not be adapted to the spiritual condition of those who hear it. God has given to every true minister the word of truth from which to select his message, and from that only must he preach. Not the fancies of his own imagination, however beautiful; nor the philosophy of his own

intellect, however cunningly devised; but the unadult-
erated truth of God, which alone can work a holy
reformation in the character of men and nations. The
message may be harsh, the tidings unwelcome, but if
they are given to us by God we cannot be silent. The
congregation may think us unceremonious and unkind,
often supposing that we wish more to alarm than to
instruct. But, even though we incur the odium of men,
we cannot but proclaim the naked truth of God in the
entirety of its meaning.

*The difficult duty which a true preacher has often
to undertake.* Jonah had to go to Nineveh and preach
against its sin, in the hope that he might work a
spiritual reformation. What a difficult and, apparently,
unequal task, for one good man to have to contend
with such a mass of wickedness. In that city there
were all classes of individuals,— soldiers and sailors,
combined for the varied enterprises of industry and
toil. And we know from the history of our own naval
and military ports, the sins that would be likely to
attain in a city like Nineveh. It was against such a
condition of things that Jonah was to preach. Surely
this would be an unthankful task in which even the
most sanguine could expect but little success. People,
as a rule, do not appreciate the difficulty of ministerial
labour. They do not consider that we have to deal
with mind and soul, that we cannot force men to be
good. If we, in this comparatively small city, surrounded by many ministers of various denominations,
appear so to be lost in its population and sin, that we
can hardly make any impression on its life, how difficult
must have been the work of the solitary Prophet thus

to influence the heart and instrumentally remove the degeneracy of that vast people. Taking this view of the matter, must we not wonder at his success, and are we not warranted in regarding it as equally miraculous with the preservation of Jonah within the belly of the great fish ? For, truly, both were alike unprecedented and designed by that Power which only can preserve the life of man, and work the moral improvement of national character.

Lastly, in this verse we have *preaching recognized as a means of moral improvement.* " Arise, go unto Nineveh, that great city, and *preach* unto it." There is a great force in the truth as preached. Books are all very well in their place, but they cannot rival the utility of the pulpit. Volumes of good pamphlets might have been sent into Nineveh, but they would not have had the happy effect produced by the oral persuasion of Jonah. In the human voice quivering with deep emotion, in the eye, tearful with genuine pity, and in the pleading attitude of the earnest preacher, there is found an appeal unequalled for its pathos and power.

So Jonah arose, and went unto Nineveh, according to the word of the Lord. Now Nineveh was an exceeding great city of three days' journey.*—*Verse* 3.

We read this announcement with very great joy, because we cannot but feel that a man like Jonah ought to obey God. He is not of feeble manhood, naturally inclined to indolence or sloth; but is strong, full of

---

*This expression may mean, either that the city was three days' journey in circuit, or that three days would be required by Jonah to make known his message in it.

enthusiasm, and therefore eminently qualified to do the right. It is always sad to see a great nature pursuing a downward course, when we instinctively feel that it is capable of noble effort. Right glad are we to turn from such a sight to the man of prophet-nature, rising from his degradation, to enter upon Prophet work. Now we find that Jonah allows the moral power of his character to flow in the right channel.

We gather from this verse *that man has power to do the right*. When Jonah set sail for Tarshish he was not moved to do so by any irrevocable decree, or by some mystic charm, which he had not the ability to resist. It was a matter of choice with him whether he would obey the Word of God or not. True, when he thought of Tarshish, some charm of fancy may have enwrapped him, presenting to his mind a happy dream that never would be realized. But he need not have been deluded by it. Jonah yielded to these magic influences until they obtained complete possession of his impulsive nature. He thought more of a pleasant sail, under sunny sky, of tranquil pleasure on a distant shore, than of the difficult mission to Nineveh. We all have, in conscious possession, the power to do right, then let us never yield to influences that would lead us to the wrong. They may be enchanting, but they are deceptive. Then let us see through such delusions and feeling that the way to Nineveh will be the happiest, be willing to move thither at the Divine call, thus escaping the voyage to Tarshish with all its peril.

This verse shows us *the folly of disobedience*. Jonah had to go to Nineveh after all, would it not have been much better had he obeyed the first command rather than the second ? Had he done so he would have avoided all the sorrow through which he had recently passed. And not only so, but his obedience would have been regarded as exemplary, and he would have been held up as a pattern to future generations. His name, instead of being associated with much that is dark, would have a bright halo surrounding it, peculiarily its own. The history of this Prophet mutually corresponds with our own experience. We, having refused to undertake a God-entrusted mission, brought years of grief upon our lives, until, after a second trial, we went to Nineveh, carrying with us the bitter memories of the past.

This verse also shows *the effectiveness of the Divine discipline.* What a great change it wrought in the thought and purpose of the runaway Prophet. How it brought him from a criminal neglect of duty to the highest performance of it.

This also shows *the ultimate meaning of the Divine discipline.* Which is not to place men in awkward circumstances merely to shew mercy and power in their deliverance. Which is not merely to give man pain and sorrow ; but so to influence his inner life that it may obediently respond to the voice of God. Looked at in this light, all heavenly discipline is happy, working out for us a far more exceeding and Eternal weight of glory.

Let us, therefore, not repine at any sorrow that may come upon our lives ; let us not grow impatient or impulsive : but calmly wait, in prayer and hope, until God shall remove the darkness, and bring forth therefrom a bright manhood ready for the great missions of life.

And Jonah began to enter into the city a day's journey, and he cried, and said, Yet forty days and Nineveh shall be overthrown. —*Verse* 4.

Now the Prophet has completed his journey. Nineveh is reached. How he travelled, and through what dangers he passed on the way we are not told. No doubt he would many times endeavour to picture to himself the city towards which he was journeying, and the work he has therein to accomplish. But how different would he find things from what he had anticipated. Soon, however, the mental picture merges into reality, for as the wearied Prophet enters into the gate of the city, the mighty walls, and majestic towers, seem to frown defiance upon him. Then, turning to the levity and splendour of that vast population, we can imagine that he would be almost dismayed at the thought of entering into conflict with it. But Jonah is altered, he is not now the coward of the first chapter, there is not the slightest token of faltering, his step is firm, and his voice rings out the words, like thunder, " Yet forty days and Nineveh shall be overthrown." There was no delay. Jonah did not wait to recruit his exhausted energy, to visit scenes of curiosity or interest in the city, or to seek the most advantageous place from which to commence his crusade. The very moment that the huge gate closed upon him he began to utter his message, from which he was not diverted either by pleasure or fear. No sooner did the words die away than they were repeated again and again in yet stronger voice. Public attention is soon attracted. The two or three friends that have casually met in the street, stay their conversation to listen to the strange announcement falling from the lips of this unknown Prophet. They cannot interpret its meaning. They look aghast at each other in amazement. There is the man surrounded by a crowd. How earnest his demeanour. Again he utters the words, "Yet forty days and Nineveh shall be overthrown." The people listen yet more attentively. They feel it. Their sins come up to their view, and they instinctively feel that what he says is true. And soon the wonderful history of this man, in prophet's attire, becomes known, which would interest his mission with additional terror. Multitudes come to see him as a curiosity, but soon return home feeling that terrible shadows are drawing over their city life. Until, at last, so deeply has he impressed the consciousness of that wicked people, that they begin to feel the need of an immediate reformation, as there are only forty days in which to avert the impending doom. The nation is moved. Its king proclaims a fast, which is universally observed.

Let us then contemplate *the ministry of Jonah as set forth by this verse*. The mission of the Prophet was followed by such unparalleled success that we ought most carefully, as people interested in the spiritual welfare of men around us, to ascertain the secret of its power. We cannot but regard this mighty reformation of character, amongst the Ninevites, as the Pentecost of the Old Testament dispensation, rivalled only by that of the New. Of course, in connecting it with the ministry of Jonah, we look at the subject in its merely human bearing. We right well know that this change of national disposition was wrought by the power of

God, but, nevertheless, this Hebrew Prophet was the medium through which it was conveyed. Therefore, as preachers, we ought to be earnest students of a ministry so undeniably productive of good and large result.

We observe that *Jonah adapted his preaching to the moral condition of those hearing it.* He was called upon to address a very large nation, civilized and refined, nevertheless debased by every description of crime, and enfeebled almost to moral decay. In it virtue was unknown, justice unheard of; passion and fraud had usurped their places, and the people appeared quite contented that they should. This state of things had lasted so long, that now they occasioned no anxiety; the folk were slumbering in their wickedness. Thus Jonah found the people amongst whom his ministry was to be exercised. How then did he deal with them? Did he talk to them on subjects altogether foreign to their condition of life? Did he prophecy smooth things unto them that their reveries might remain unbroken? No! He hurled upon their carnal tranquility the most terrible message that could possibly have been found. He threatened the city with universal destruction, and surely few of its inhabitants but would be aroused by such a cry as "Yet forty days and Nineveh shall be overthrown." Thus Jonah did not go into a metaphysical analysis of sin in its varied stages, nor did he enter upon a philosophical discussion of certain doctrines to be credited; but, assuming the wickedness of the city, he so fashioned his ministry that it should appeal to the moral consciousness of those who heard it.

Again, *the preaching of Jonah was most alarming.*

"Yet forty days and Nineveh shall be overthrown."
Surely nothing could have been more awe-inspiring to
the Ninevites than this. Here is nothing to excite their
fancy, kindle their imagination, or even to win their
sympathy. The message is stern and in apparent defiance of all their greatness and power. Naturally would
the Ninevites imagine as to who should be the means
of so great an overthrow, and some might even dare
to vaunt their prowess and courage in the event of war.
But heedless of all cavil the Prophet would again declare "Yet forty days and Nineveh shall be overthrown."
And this oft repeated threat would strike terror into
many a brave heart, and be calculated to hush the
mirth of the whole city. I should think that this is
what some people would call a "hell-fire" ministry, to
which they profess so great an objection. They prefer
that the pulpit should gather its argument from the
Cross rather than from the torments of the lost. They
consider the motive derived from the former to be more
worthy in its influence upon the human will in the
choice of good. And possibly this may be so. Nevertheless the terrors of the law are often most effective
to the rescue of moral character from eternal ruin,
especially when brought to bear upon a certain type of
disposition. And this being the case, they ought to be
pressed into service by all seeking to ameliorate the
condition of their fellow creatures. And when this is
done, by the preacher, let the marvellous good accomplished by the terrible ministry of Jonah shield him
from rebuke.

Again we observe that *the preaching of Jonah was
specific*. The subject of his discourse was the sin of

Nineveh and its connection with the doom now threatened by God. And to this he most rigidly adhered,
never allowing imagination to carry beyond, nor a
brilliant rhetoric to betray him from it. His sermon
was pointed. One thought had permeated his entire
nature. He felt his position and the all importance of
the theme entrusted to his care for the moral good of
Nineveh. Hence he had not the disposition to direct
public attention to any other of minor import. Jonah
knew that the great mass of people about him were
on the very brink of ruin, and therefore could not
afford madly to sport with their eternal destiny. We
think that the ministry of to-day may gather much
instruction here. Our sermons are too discursive, we
often rove from the grand theme of the Gospel, just to
pluck a few flowers, that do not add beauty, devoid of
holy fragrance, and that very soon fade. This is not
the way to influence character. Moral evil is a dire
speciality, and as such must be treated by the pulpit.
The truly called, and Divinely inspired minister must
feel that sin is one of the greatest and most grim fac-
tors of human life, and that therefore he cannot afford
to meet it indirectly. He must address it in its dire
individuality ; and in proportion as he realises the fact
that souls, attendant on his ministry, are exposed to its
future retribution, he will do so. This thought, imparting
a sense of deep responsibility, will inspire him with a
simplicity and earnestness that must lend additional
force to his pulpit effort.

Further, *the preaching of Jonah was short.* If the
cry found in this verse constituted the sermon of the
Prophet, then indeed it was brief. No traveller would

be able to complain of tediousness. Neither would anyone be long detained to hear the tidings of future woe. Jonah did not hide the magnitude of Nineveh's crime in long sentences, but laid it open in few simple words. Nor could this brief method of address fail to inspire those who heard it with deep solemnity. In this respect also, our modern pulpit might wisely imitate the example of Jonah. Our sermons in the present day are much too long. This destroys their effectiveness, interrupting the reciprocal play of sympathy between the pulpit and the pew. Spiritual influence is a very subtle thing, and requires the utmost care that its effect upon the mind may be intensified and preserved. Spiritual good is much more dependent on these little matters than we are inclined to admit. If people are tired with sitting, or are worn out by a long monotonous sermon, there can be very little hope of doing them good. We want, as preachers, to think less of the human agency, by which souls are to be saved, and more of the Divine. Long sermons are often the result of vanity. Let us, then, remember the short homily of Jonah, and the great good in which it resulted to Nineveh.

We cannot but observe *that Jonah was a good open-air preacher*. He appears to have had quite a natural aptitude for the work. He possessed a *good voice*, which is no small help in such an employment. And better still, he was not afraid to use it, but *cried* "Yet forty days and Nineveh shall be overthrown." Also, *he was courageous*. He was not afraid of any who might be passing in the street. He feared not the violence of an unruly mob ; nor did the indifference of the refined move him, nor yet the invective of the sceptic. Defying all opposition, he took his stand in the throughfares of the city to preach a sermon in no way flattering to those who heard it. The church could do with men of this class to-day.

Nor can we look over the fact *that the open-air preaching of Jonah became the human instrumentality of a great spiritual revival.* This remarkable man might have preached in one of the sanctuaries of Nineveh for months and yet not have realized the success of this one day's mission in the open-air. True, his late adventure with the great fish, his nationality, and his power as a true hearted preacher, would have gained him popularity. Thousands would have flocked to the church in which he ministered, still there would have remained multitudes untouched by him. As there are always plenty in a large city who would not be attracted from their indolence and squalor by the best preacher that has ever lived, not even if he were to rise from the dead to deliver the sermon. Thus we cannot but see that open-air preaching meets a great want in the church life of to-day. It is the only way by which the masses of the people can be reached, and brought into contact with spiritual truth. And is it not a matter of history that most great revivals of religion, with which we are acquainted, have been preceded by it? We cannot but associate the revival of the eighteenth century with the open-air preaching of Whitfield, and Wesley. Let us then, as Christian churches, encourage this department of labour, hoping that in our own times it may be followed by results as glorious as in the past, and so happy in their bearing upon the eternal destiny of men.

Having now reviewed the style and method of Jonah's ministry, *we wish briefly to contemplate the punishment threatened thereby.* "Yet forty days and Nineveh shall be destroyed." This message was Divinely communicated to Jonah, and was at the very basis of his mission. *The punishment threatened was humiliating.* "*Nineveh* shall be overthrown." It was not a small town, almost unknown to the world, that was to be destroyed, but one of the largest and most celebrated cities then in existence. Nineveh had fortresses, and warriors brave, but here was threatened a catastrophe against which she had no protection. *This punishment was pitiable.* For a city of such grand buildings and memorials, of such splendid art, and magnificent genius, to be smitten to the dust,—the very thought of it appeals to all our feelings of pity. *The punishment was terrible.* "Nineveh shall be *overthrown.*" Not merely was it to be terrified by the temporary shock of an earthquake ; it was to be completely destroyed. All would be left in ruins, and amidst a fallen mass of stone, relicts of a former grandeur, there would be no trace of design or beauty ; everything is to be hushed in the silence of a universal death. To this only could the Ninevites look forward from the ministry of Jonah. *This punishment was soon to take place.* "Yet forty days." Not long were the Ninevites forewarned of their danger. The shortness of the term to intervene, between the preaching of Jonah and the overthrow of the city, would be an additional motive to solemnity.

Is not this ancient picture typical of our own moral

condition?   Are we not many of us living in a habit of
sin ?   Our lives are unholy,—at variance with every
principle of rectitude.   Before us is a future, perhaps
not forty days from our tread.   A thousand solemn,
simple ministries are sent to warn us of our peril; but
they are, as yet, unheeded.   We would press them upon
your consciences now, with renewed energy, hoping that
the result may be as cheerful as that witnessed in the
history of Nineveh.

So the people of Nineveh believed God, and proclaimed a fast,
and put on sackcloth, from the greatest of them even to the least of
them.—*Verse* 5.

We now witness the results of Jonah's ministry,
under the blessing of God, in the repentance and
humiliation of the Ninevites. *We regard this repentance
as most readily manifested by the middle and lower ranks
of Society.* " So the people of Nineveh believed God."
And in the following verses we have a distinct reference
to the king and his nobles as being the last to hear of
Jonah's message.   It is probable that they lived away
from the public thoroughfares, and consequently did
not know anything about the appeal of Jonah to the
city.   The aristocracy would not be prepared for his
visit; and who would dare to disturb their quiet by
communicating the street cries of a vagrant enthusiast.
However, passing from this incident to history in
general, it is worthy of note that nearly all the great
movements of the past have been more readily taken
up by the poorer classes.   The mission of Christ was
more readily welcomed by the poor.   Just so was it

with the great Reformation; and, in our own times, nearly all the philanthropic measures of the Government have had more willing acceptance with the populace. Nor can we altogether understand the reason of this. Our aristocracy cannot plead the same excuse as that mentioned for the king of Nineveh and his nobles. They have not been ignorant of these great enterprises, on the contrary, they have often opposed them. Probably they are naturally more conservative than their inferiors, and are not quite so quick in their instinctive appreciation of the useful. It is not that the poorer grades of society are supremely gifted with intelligence, and can therefore more readily discern the worth of events; nor is it altogether that they are more credulous or superstitious; but we attribute it greatly to the fact that they are more enthusiastic and spontaneous in their method of life, and hence are more inclined to speculate in the new. We also believe that the instinct of the poor, as a rule, is very true to that which is good. Hence, before the higher classes have overcome the indolence occasioned by their surroundings, and have broken through the conventionality of their life, the poorer have half completed the work. We hope that soon this reproach, whatever may be its cause, will be removed from those holding high positions in our country.

We regard this repentance as prompted by a motive every way the most worthy. " So the people of Nineveh believed God." Hence, in this reformation of character, they were not animated by a selfish desire for their own safety, rather than by a disinterested wish for purity of disposition. *Their repentance embraced an earnest belief in the Divine Existence.* They abandoned their idols for the worship of the true God, as the sailors had done in the first chapter. This is the first indication of their recovery from heathen darkness. Probably the miraculous history of the Prophet had deepened this thought within the mind of the Ninevites. His life would make them feel as though they were in the very sanctuary of God.

But the ministry of Jonah not only made known the existence of God to the Ninevites, but also His relation to the moral life of man. It gave them to see that the Divine existence was not merely a theory to be credited, but a solemn fact underlying all human life in its every phase of being. This was the chief element in their repentance. It gave them to view their sin in a new light, not only in itself, nor even in its bearing towards each other, but its deeper relation to the Infinite. It should be the constant aim of our ministry to awaken men to a true consciousness of their moral nearness to God; then they would soon repent, and find in His love the undisturbed hour of their souls.

Such a belief in God is the secret of all true soul-reformation. A nation must get proper notions of God, deep seated in its heart, before its life can be pure. This is the great need of France in our own day. The Senate may gather all its genius, and issue laws of the highest order, but they will not Christianize the people. A nation may educate the masses, but this will only increase their facility for doing wrong. There are springs of evil in the human soul, that cannot be touched by legal enactments, or scholastic discipline. A true and abiding recognition of God, as the supreme power of

life, as ever near to the soul, is the only worthy motive
of a true repentance.

Further, we observe *that in this repentance the Ninevites did not give undue prominence to external ceremony.*
They did not content themselves with fasting, or wear-
ing sackcloth, but they also believed God. Hence,
underneath the outward appearance of sorrow, there
was a recognition of Divine principle, without which
everything else would have been meaningless and vain.
It is not enough for penitent sinners merely to show
regret in the external demeanour, there must be an
inward consciousness of having grieved God, else the
sackcloth and ashes are but empty mockery. Thus
what a great change has come over the life of this vast
city. Instead of revelry there is prayer; instead of
wanton luxury there is fasting; and instead of gay
apparel there is sackcloth. Truly, nothing could have
wrought such a transformation in the character of these
Ninevites, but a heart-faith in the Divine existence.

*The repentance of these people was accompanied by a
fast.* It would appear that the king did not know that
the people had, independently of himself, proclaimed a
fast. This fast would have a beneficial effect upon the
Ninevites, it would tend to deepen their repentance, to
break them away from their gaiety, and to give deep
solemnity to their conduct. This, however, they did
not regard as an essential element in their grief, being
merely helpful to it. It was a token of humiliation,
and as such they viewed it. From this we gather that
fasting may serve very important purposes in the religious life of men and cities, and therefore ought not to
be disregarded. While there is much about this national

repentance that is temporary and local, there is far
more that is Divine and enduring,—eminently worthy
of universal imitation.

*We regard this national repentance as conducted
throughout with the highest order.* " From the greatest
of these even to the least of them." Although the
people acted independently of the king in proclaiming
a fast, there is no record of any insubordination on their
part, but of deep earnestness in their determination to
commence a new life. And, considering the deep conviction that had taken hold of their hearts, and the
alarming nature of the threatened doom, we almost
wonder how this national humiliation could have been
conducted after so orderly a manner. We do not read of
any evil-disposed person taking advantage of the general sorrow, to disturb the public peace by riot. And,
notwithstanding the awful consciousness that had settled upon the mind of the city, there are no instances
of suicidal despair. In this scene, so radiant with the
tokens of Divine mercy, everything appears orderly
and quiet. Seldom do the pages of history record so
great a revolution carried out so calmly. The hush of
another life has come upon Nineveh. But soon its
silence will be broken by the glad anthems of a people
freed from the curse of their long continued wickedness,
and delivered from the doom announced by the Hebrew
Prophet.

*Thus we find that a true revival of moral character
may be conducted without uproar and confusion.* The
deep feeling of the heart may vent itself in tears—but
they are silent. The sin convicted may make known
the wicked secrets of their past life in prayer,—but

these can be whispered. Not that we wish at such a
time to prevent the out-flow of the soul by conventional formality. The soul must have its Niagara. But
even then its rush and roar may be harmonious. There
need not be confusion. Here then is a pattern for our
modern revival gatherings.

Lastly, *we must regard this repentance as associated
with the ministry of Jonah.* We have to link the great
concern of the Ninevites for their spiritual welfare, and
the proclamation of a fast, with the ministry of that once
runaway, but now obedient Prophet. We speak after the
manner of men; for behind that Prophet there was a
holier, a diviner power, that made him the medium of
its operation. That power was God. We cannot think
too much about the success of this Old Testament
ministry. *It was marvellous.* Jonah had no one to
help him in his mission. He was alone. He wrought
no miracles before the people; he had not the ability
given him to do so, and otherwise he could not. He
made no pretensions to personal authority, wealth, or
birth, by which he might gain influence with the multitude. He appeared as a humble Prophet with the
singular message, " Yet forty days and Nineveh shall
be overthrown." And yet it is with this ministry that
we have to connect so great a revival of national purity.
It was unparalleled. Noah preached under similar circumstances for one hundred and twenty years, and yet
did not produce the result here recorded. Lot preached
to the Sodomites until his righteous soul was grieved
with their indifference. Even the ingathering of converts on the day of Pentecost is not so wonderful as
the success of Jonah. Then Christ had been sowing

the seeds of His life, thoughts and words, for some
time; and, in scattering the precious grain of the
Kingdom, he had also been assisted by His disciples.
Hence, prior to the revival of Pentecost, there was
prepared a church to receive and welcome, and aid its
effectiveness. But the streets of Nineveh were not
favoured with the incarnate presence of Christ, followed
by twelve disciples; and when the consciousness of
sin had taken hold upon the inhabitants, there was no
friendly influence abroad to conserve and enhance its
progress. There were no Godly people praying in the
"upper room" in Nineveh, upon which the sinful multitude could fall back for direction. Jonah was the
only Godly man amongst them, and perhaps he was
hardly prepared for this result, or to act in this emergency. This was truly a national out-burst of feeling,
aroused by the preaching of one man, and as such is
unparalleled. *It was happy.* About this there can be
no two opinions. All the great resources of the city
are now to be consecrated to the right end. Its social
life will be purified. Its commerce will be upraised
from the degradation into which it had fallen. All the
enterprises of the city will have a new impetus given
to them. A true reformation of character has thrown
its charm on all around, and, certainly, nothing can
surpass its beauty. Fraud and passion are no longer
to hold the sway of the public mind, but honesty and
purity. What a happy exchange! And thus this
mighty city that was a few hours ago trooping as fast
as possible to hell, is now marching gladly to heaven.
What a change in its history! and brought about by
the preaching of this one man!

Thus we see what a beneficial effect a true ministry has upon the civil life of a people. As Nineveh was thus refined in its civil life by the preaching of Jonah, so England to-day owes the strength of her commerce, the purity of her morality, and the happiness of her domestic life, in a large extent, to the ministries of her numerous pulpits. No one can question that many severe catastrophies have been averted from us, as a nation, by the effort which they have produced upon the moral disposition of men.

Let us, then, pause to compare the success of our modern pulpit with this ministry of ancient times. Not that we would do so in desponding mood, or in disatis-fied spirit, but with the hope that it may lead us to more Christly pulpit effort for the spiritual welfare of those around us. While we cannot but regard the success of the Prophet, at Nineveh, as somewhat mira-culous, yet *how is it that the ministry of to-day does not even approximate to a like happy result?* We sorrow-fully admit that the achievements of the pulpit in our own times are not so glorious as that in which Jonah was privileged to take part. But the fault is not altogether due to a deteriorated ministry. We believe that the pulpits of the world were never filled with hearts more loyal to Christ, and truer to the interests of humanity, than to-day. How then is this lack of success to be explained? We believe that *it is greatly attributable to the increased power which refined sin has gained over the public mind.* Society does not generally run to the extreme of debauchery, as in the days of Nineveh, but has enconsed itself behind a cold morality far more difficult to remove. People addicted to violent excess know that they are wrong, while many whose lives are outwardly true, persuade themselves that they are right and safe. The former are far more susceptible to the power of an earnest ministry than the latter, and as our sanctuaries are generally attended by this class of hearers, our success is not so great, and cannot compare with that of this Jewish Prophet, whose appeals fell upon an already conscience stricken city. "Verily I say unto you, That the publicans and the harlots go into the kingdom of God before you."

> For word came unto the king of Nineveh, and he arose from his throne, and he laid aside his robe from him, and covered him with sackcloth and sat in ashes.—*Verse* 6.

We see pourtrayed in this verse *the general seclusion of a monarch's life*. That there should have been all this stir in the city, occasioned by the preaching of Jonah, and the king, ignorant of it for so long a time, seems almost a matter of surprise to us. This can only be accounted for by the secluded character of his royal life. It seems to be thought desirable that monarchs should be excluded from the rush and toil of every-day business. Hence they betake themselves to more sequestered scenes, and thus it comes to happen that there may be enterprises carried on within their realm of which they are entirely ignorant, yea, even antagonistic to their rule. We think that the lives and influence of kings would be much more beneficial, and effective if this cold isolation were overcome, and a mutual sympathy created between them and their subjects, by an unreserved community of life. Not that we would divest the kingly office of its importance, on the contrary, we would render it more attractive to the public mind. Seclusion is only necessary for deformity, and tends more to promote rumour and superstition, than to encourage truth ; while the intimate association of a monarch with the affairs of the nation he governs, tends to inspire with confidence, and gives an impetus to everything with which he is connected.

Nevertheless, we cannot but remark that, although the king of Nineveh lived in this seclusion, *he was a king truly kingly*. The manner in which he acted during the national humiliation abundantly proves this. When the tidings, that Jonah had communicated to the city, were brought to him, he did not put on airs of dignity, but immediately concurred in the popular wish for a fast. He did not question the authority of the Prophet, or exhibit signs of displeasure at his having disturbed the public peace ; but at once arose " from his throne, and laid aside his robe, and covered himself with sackcloth, and sat in ashes." This description of grief belongs to the time in which the king lived, and especially to the nation over which he reigned. This outward symbolism of inward regret has past away. However, we are glad to find it in connection with this narrative of kingly humiliation, as a token of something holier. Never was the king of Nineveh more fit to be its king than now. Never in battle, or achievement, did he win the title royal so much as in this conquest over self. In his weakness he is exalted. He has removed all tokens of empire and pomp. They only reminded him of his sin ; of voluptuousness and pride ; and, this being the case, they are little better than mockery under his present circumstances.

*These outward signs of power and influence only serve
to deepen the contrast between the king's greatness and the
ruin threatened by the Prophet.* Hence he orders them to
be removed. It is little use to decorate a dead body with
flowers and emblems of joy and life. Would that men
to-day, under like circumstances, would imitate the
example of the heathen king. There are thousands
walking our streets arrayed in all that wealth can buy,
and others inhabiting fine mansions, whose social circumstances are a complete satire upon their inner consciousness of future woe. The germs of a nearing hell
are growing within their lives, and promise soon to
break forth in grim fruit; but there the lordlings are, in
pomp and grandeur, as though all within were pure
and happy. How much better and consistent would it
be, if they had the sense and conscience to exchange
these outward symbols of wealth for the sackcloth of
repentance; again to resume them when the inner life
should respond to their happiness. There is nothing
wrong in the throne and the robe, only they do not befit
the threatened future of a wicked spirit.

This king was truly kingly *because he listened to a
communication respecting the moral character of his subjects.* The king of Nineveh regarded the account given
to him of the preaching of Jonah and its connection
with the sin of his people. He even invested it with
his royal authority, and instead of issuing a series of
civil enactments, fell back upon the awakened spiritual
instincts of the city and urged it to repent. We cannot but think that monarch's in our own day might
gather a lesson here. That in certain national crises it
may be far better for them to enforce the pulpit minis-

trations of the land, and to seek the moral reformation
of the country thereby, than to assemble their Parlia-
ments, and issue laws that, probably, do not touch the
real cause of threatened punishment. It is surprising
to read how frequently kings employ secondary agencies for the welfare of their subjects, when the spiritual
and primary would be much more effective. In fact,
if nations would but pay a greater regard to the Divine
motive, bringing it into truer contact with every
phase of life, we believe that civil law, and all its
consequent auxiliaries, would be almost entirely super-
seded, and the Bible would become, in a very real sense,
the statute book of the nations. The spirit and manner in which the king of Nineveh received the citizens
who informed him of Jonah's mission in the city is
every way worthy of praise and imitation. He listened
with the utmost sympathy to their communication. We
cannot tell who informed him of the ministry of Jonah
in Nineveh; whether he was waited upon by one individual, or by a number of persons. Probably, the
latter, as they would be better able to urge their case
if necessity required. But there was no need for
argument on their part. The king, as they had done,
instinctively felt the message to be true, and Divinely
communicated to the city. He therefore felt that he
was one with those around him. He did not treat the
matter lightly, with the coldness of state officialism, but
as though he was personally concerned in it. Perhaps
he was conscience stricken. He felt that his life had not
been so pure as it ought to have been, and that therefore the wickedness of the people was partially due to
his example. For nothing has such a deteriorating effect

upon the general morality of a nation as the influence of a depraved court. Then sin is made respectable, and is invested with the sanction of high life, which in the sight of many would rob it of all criminality.

But deputations in these days do not always meet with as sympathetic a reception as that given to these citizens who waited upon this ancient king. When a number of individuals go to any state dignitary to make known a wrong, or to seek legislation that will enhance the public welfare, they are generally met with rigid formality, reaching almost to indifference, and, at the most, are only promised careful and respectful attention; whereas, if only the conventionality of the occasion was overcome, and a freedom of speech allowed, important interests might be greatly benefited. We think, then, that state officials, in this respect, may learn much from the conduct of this ancient king of Nineveh.

Again, a king truly kingly *is one who will himself set an example of moral reformation to his people in times of degeneracy.* The king of Nineveh not merely received the tidings announced by Jonah, but made them the motive of his personal conduct. He commanded a national humiliation, and repentance in which he himself joined with great propriety. He laid aside the tokens of his office, and wealth, and sought the Divine forgiveness; and thus the king's devout behaviour, at this time, was indeed worthy of his position, and would tend to give the proclamation an importance and authority that otherwise it could not have had. There was no display about this national humiliation, all was intensely real and earnest; the one desire of the city was for the mercy of God.

From all this we gather that *that king is wisest and best who is most sensitive to the indications of Divine Providence in reference to events pertaining to his realm.* Prior to any special calamity God generally sends a premonition to the nation He is about to visit. He may send a Prophet to announce in clear language its future overthrow, or He may commission some other agency equally emphatic. Hence a monarch should be always on the outlook for the moral significance of events passing around them, that no Jonah may be allowed to visit their city without being made the inspiration of national reform.

And he caused it to be proclaimed and published through Nineveh by the decree of the king and his nobles, saying, Let neither man nor beast, herd nor flock, taste anything ; let them not feed, nor drink water.—*Verse 7.*

In this verse we have *the ministry of Jonah brought under state patronage.* The message of Jonah, respecting the future of Nineveh, that had made such a deep impression upon the public mind, is now taken into consideration by the king and his nobles. They unitedly hold a council, and determine to act immediately upon the tidings just communicated to them, hence they announce a national humiliation. Thus soon did the ministry of the Prophet gain the sanction and authority of the court, and there can be little doubt that this was one great means of its extensive usefulness.

The unity that seems to have pervaded their council on this matter is every way worthy of recognition and commendation. Perhaps there were not quite so **many**

religious sects in those days as in these, and hence this
council would not find it so difficult to agree on the
question of state patronage, as a like convention would
now. And, had it not been animated by a strong
feeling of oneness; had it not intensely felt the
responsibility of its position, we can easily imagine
that there might have been serious contention amongst
these nobles, as the question was not whether they
should affix their sanction to the advancement of any
then existing and national form of worship, but whether
they would commend, to the notice of their subjects,
a religion entirely new, and which had been introduced to them in so strange a manner. We could
not have wondered if several had been found to contend for their ancient system of idolatry. But such
was not the case. All opposition to the God of the
Prophet was hushed by the mysterious impressions
made upon their hearts by the tidings of their common doom. The deliberations of *this council were
unprejudiced*. Its members felt that candour was necessary, and this they were prepared to manifest. They
knew they could not afford to spend time in talking
about, and contending for, the comparative worth of
existing religious institutions. There was an imperative
necessity that their only thought should be directed to
the general deliverance of the city from its threatened
future, apart from any mere party question. *The deliberations of this council were solemn*. The members
of this assembly did not feel as though they were the
peers of the realm, because they were so humiliated by
a remembrance of their sin. They regarded Jonah as,
morally, the king of Nineveh, and to any suggestion

made by him they would readily have paid defference. And, thus abased before God, they prepared to divest their convention of all political bearing, that looking up to Him, it might devise the truest means for safety from the threatened overthrow.

We cannot but contrast the spirit and action of this ancient council with that found in our national assembly to-day. If any subject is introduced into our Parliament bordering on the "religious question," that is quite sufficient to excite prejudice, and to arouse animosity. Hence the great difficulty experienced by statesmen in striving to legislate on these supremely important affairs. And frequently, through this bitter sectism, the most philanthropic measures are lost to the country. Would it not be far more catholic and worthy if men, merging their distinctive theological opinions, would combine in one right royal proclamation for the moral good of the nation. It is high time that all these religious controversies in our senate were ended, that a united unprejudiced influence may be brought to bear upon these evils, that have so long affected our land, and that cannot but attract the displeasure of God.

Let us then look at *the purpose for which the king and the nobles of Nineveh gave the sanction of the state to the ministry of Jonah.* And, in this respect, they are a pattern for all monarchs and their advisers. They urged the nation to credit the ministry of Jonah and to repent. Surely, never did the supreme power of. Nineveh lend its sanction to any enterprise more noble. And if state patronage to-day meant anything like this, the acknowledgement of earnest ministries, working

for the repentance, and moral improvement of the
people, every true man would rejoice in it. Whereas,
instead of this, it is, in our own day, having quite
a contrary effect upon our national character; enhancing the spread of Popery, conniving at Ritualism, and freezing the warm impulses of our religious
life, by the cold channels through which they flow.
Of this the populace is becoming conscious, how can
we wonder then that they should cry out against it. We
are sometimes told that men cannot be made good by
Act of Parliament, and no doubt this is partially true;
but we see from this narrative that kings, and those in
authority over us, can do a great deal for the spiritual
good of those placed under them by the power of civil
law. Let the State but give her patronage to a general
revival of true piety, let her be as real in her motive,
and as simple in her effort, as was the ancient king of
Nineveh, and it would be beyond the power of man to
predict what would be the eternal result. As spiritual
feeling was awakened in Nineveh by this proclamation
of the king, so, no doubt, the appeal of our State
officials would find a response in many conscious-
stricken hearts to whom it might come.

*The decree of this council was universal in its appli-
cation.* Not merely were all the people to join in this
humiliation announced, but even the cattle were to be
covered with sackcloth, and left without their accus-
tomed food. Thus would Nineveh be everywhere surrounded by the tokens of her guilt, and the bleating
of the sheep, and the bellowing of the cattle, would
tend to deepen the conviction of sin, as did the crow-
ing of the cock in the case of repentant Peter.

The issue of this proclamation was the wisest thing they could have done. Had they vaunted their prowess, continued in their sin, and defied the lonely messenger of God, a more speedy destruction, or a more terrible woe might have come upon them. But this contrition for sin attracted the Divine compassion, and brought from heaven the mercy that was needed to shield and save so vast a people. Let then every impenitent sinner learn from this page that humiliation before God on account of sin is the truest wisdom, while delay may be but a synonym for death.

But let man and beast be covered with sackcloth, and cry mightily unto God: yea, let them turn everyone from his evil way, and from the violence that is in their hands.—*Verse 8.*

In this verse *we have Nineveh seeking the removal of her threatened overthrow.* And we cannot but remark the means the Ninevites employed, and the spirit they cultivated, in order to obtain its removal. If, instead of heathens, they had been apostate Christians, having had the Divine light of truth shed upon their hearts, though now living in darkness, they could not have pursued a better or more worthy method of conduct. So truly do the intuitions of the human soul lead it to that which is godly, especially where there is the faintest desire to seek the pure in character. There is within the most wicked nature a germ of something good, covered over, it may be, by much that is unholy; but, nevertheless, it is there, and will probably one day work itself to the surface in fervent contrition toward God. One ray from the Cross, gleaming into such a manhood, can touch that germ into the dominant power of the soul. Thus was it with the history of Nineveh. Amidst all their impiety and idolatry, there was yet a lingering something that was the preservation and hope of their life, and this, appealed to by the ministry of Jonah, and intensified by the gentle, but quickening influences of heaven, manifested itself in a disposition to repent. Then, as there is no life so desperate but has a few seeds of good within its circle, happy if they are developed by such earnest, heaven-blessed ministries, as that of the Prophet's.

The narrative informs us that *Nineveh recognised prayer as a means for the removal of its threatened punishment.* " And cry mightily unto God." In doing this there can be little doubt but that they were prompted by an almost intuitive desire to gain the assistance of a Divine power in their extremity. But, instead of seeking this in their idols, they turn to Jehovah, lately made known to them by the Prophet. The soul must pray in trouble, if not to the true Deity, to some fancied one. And is not the deep naturalness of worship at such times, a token that there is, in an unknown manner, a connection between the supreme Being and the future events of our life? Does not this intuitive belief, as manifested in this narrative, controvert the assertion of infidelity, that God cannot influence an impending future in harmony with our desire, and that He will not be moved to do so by our prayer? Men announce the stability of law, both physical and moral, and say that the present condition of things is the result of a continuous process during ages which cannot be altered,

without all the minute agencies of the past being per-
verted, which is an impossibility ; and that, therefore,
our prayers must be ineffectual.* We have placed the
working of God in the moral realm of being, by the
side of His operations in the sphere of the material
universe, because both are considered alike inflexible
in their laws. We wonder that learned men can pen such
sentences as those quoted below. Is not prayer as
much a law in these two spheres of life, as the law of atmospherical influences, gravitation, or the observable
connection between sin and misery ? And is not the,
so-called, constitution of nature adapted equally to
the working of one as the other ? And, such being
the case, what can be more reasonable than for us to
avail ourselves of the existence of this law of prayer,
and, consistently with it, to ask God, to protect us from
impending doom of whatever kind. Unless we are
believers in fate, or regard the Divine Being as devoid
of all power to influence the world He has created we
cannot but regard prayer as a means of averting anticipated woe. And that God heard the united prayer
of Nineveh, shows our reasoning to be in harmony with
the revelation of inspired truth. It is strange that, in
the recent controversy on this topic, no objector to
the efficacy of prayer, in the moral and physical realms
of life, has attempted to mention the various scripture

---

*When we pray, then, that God would cause the rain to cease, we
are asking one of those two things — either that He would work a
miracle for us, or; if we abjure that wish, that He would change, not
circumstances as they exist at present, but all the natural phenomena
which have existed on the globe, which is manifestly absurd." —
Stopford A. Brooke, *Christ in Modern Life,* page 135.

records that show its power. This silence is either a testimony to their rejection of scripture fact, or else to their inability to explain it consistently with their own philosophy. For, certainly, before prayer, as our hope in God, can be removed, these histories must be nullified. The Ninevites believed that not only prayer influenced God, but also that it would avert the calamity with which they were threatened. And the sequel of the narrative proves that they were warranted in their creed. Let the wise men of to-day learn true wisdom from the simplicity and sorrow of these ancient people, for vain must be the philosophy that is antagonistic to such an experience as theirs.

Their prayer was rendered effective by deep contrition. The Ninevites did not pray because of the peril to which they were exposed, but because of the guilt of which they were deeply conscious. Their prayers were not animated by a selfish desire for safety, but by an earnest wish for pardon. Thus they found acceptance with God, who, in answer thereto, removed the sin of Nineveh and its threatened penalty. True contrition of soul lends to prayer a pathos and power that nothing else can so eminently impart. Let us see that it is not wanting in our devotion.

Their prayer was rendered effective by true earnestness. "And cry mightily unto God." Not that loud prayer is necessarily earnest. There is often much noise in worship where there is but little real fervour. True, in the streets and homes of Nineveh there may have been loud cries to God for help, uttered by contrite hearts. But behind all this, in many great natures, citizens of that threatened city, there would be silent, unuttered devotion, as sincere and earnest as that accompanied by such violent expressions of agony. And, no doubt, the great strength of Nineveh at this time would lay in the unwhispered emotion of these grief-stricken worshippers. So, in the sanctuary where no voice is heard, there may be as fervent appeals to God as though many were praying audibly. True earnestness is in the soul, and not in the external demeanour or the voice. And with this earnestness the people of Nineveh were eminently gifted.

Their prayer was rendered effective by being offered to the true God. " And cry mightily unto God." The Ninevites might have been sorrowful, they might have been earnest in prayer, but unless their grief and devotion had been of Godward tendency, the one would not have been removed, the other would not have been answered. Had they prayed to their own idols for immunity from the threatened overthrow, there would have been none to answer nor any to regard. But in the Deity made known to them by Jonah, they had found a better source of protection; hence they forgot their heathen lives; the past associations of their idolatry, in intimate communion with Jehovah. God is the only worthy object of our devotion, and if presented elsewhere, it will be utterly useless. Let us then in circumstances of peril, make the spirit and prayer of the Ninevites a pattern for our own.

Further, we see that *the Ninevites urged a reformation of moral character as a means for the removal of their threatened punishment.* " Yea, let them turn, every one from his evil way, and from the violence that is in their hands." *This reformation was truly*

necessary. It was necessary to harmonise with the
prayers offered by the Ninevites. Their petitions
would have been of very little service to them unless
they had been accompanied by this resolution. Of
course not. This proved the reality of their supplications, and rendered them acceptable to God. And
besides, their wickedness was such that it could not
longer be allowed to continue; hence, if they did not
reform, destruction was inevitable. This they no
doubt felt. *This reformation was determined.* Their
sin was not merely one isolated act, but it had
become habit; and hence would require a firm will to
resist it successfully. No half-hearted endeavour would
be sufficient, but all the enthusiasm of the soul would
be needed. No doubt their spiritual powers would be
greatly impaired by the manner in which they had
been subordinated to evil, and would not be capable of
the highest moral force; nevertheless, that they are
equal to the occasion, is demonstrated by the narrative.
All effort to overcome the momentum that our lives have
gathered from the sin of the past, must be thoroughly
determined, or it will fail. *This reformation was truly
noble.* A foolish spirit of bravado might have led the
Ninevites to meet the future punishment with boldness,
and this many would have applauded as courageous.
But the truest courage is ever consistent with the truest
moral good. And they manifested it in their determination to repent. It was a courage that overcame self
and pride, and that achieved a result most happy for
the city. Let us never be ashamed to amend our
conduct, and to make known our intention to those
around us, as herein we display a nobility of soul that

will gain admiration. *This reformation was deeply significant.* It indicated that they were conscious of their wrong doing, and that they were ready to confess it before God. It intimated humility. They did not unfold any deed of goodness that, as a nation, they might have done; such as relieving the oppressed, or condemning the guilty; they acknowledged that they were as bad as the ministry of Jonah would imply. They did not try to excuse their sin, but with true sincerity of heart confessed it. *This was done individually.* The Ninevites did not loose sight of their individuality in their nationality. Though they had lived together under one civil rule, and were intimately associated in the relationships and duties of life, they felt that they stood before God in their own personality, and accordingly made their confession of sin. And so must it be with us. No matter how intricate and binding the relationships of our earthly life, they must all fall to the ground when the higher life of the soul is brought into the immediate presence of the Infinite. At that time the penitent soul must stand alone; yea, not alone, but accompanied by its sins, to receive the mercy it requires.

In all this we have the evidence of a genuine repentance. If they had not acknowledged their violence as continued through a long series of years, there would have been no token of true contrition. There might have been sorrow, but sorrow is not necessarily repentant; it may be selfish and despairing, rather than purifying and consoling, only when accompanied by a reformed character is it the latter, and then only is it real. This God requires of those who come to seek His mercy; hence there is always a deep necessity for it.

Who can tell if God will turn and repent, and turn away from his fierce anger, that we perish not.—*Verse* 9.

These words form part of the proclamation issued by the king of Nineveh, and are eminently worthy of careful study. In them we have expressed a heathen's idea of the long-suffering and mercy of God. They contain a supposition *that the threatened overthrow may yet be averted by a reformation of moral character on the part of the Ninevites.* " Who can tell if God will turn and repent." Why did the king of Nineveh and his nobles doubt as to the execution of the threatened doom ? Had they any reason for so doing ? *Was the ministry of Jonah lenient ?* Surely there was not much hope to be gathered from a ministry whose only cry was " Yet forty days and Nineveh shall be overthrown." Not one ray of mercy could break forth upon the nation from a cloud so dark as this. And as there was little in the message of Jonah to betoken the mercy of God, there was even less in his abrupt demeanour. From the petulance of the Prophet we see that he had no desire for the salvation of the Ninevites ; not that he altogether wished their ruin, but he feared lest his denunciation of woe should turn out to be untrue. And no doubt this feeling would be evident to those by whom he was surrounded. They would regard him as the herald of their overthrow. How then could such a presence lead the affrighted Ninevites to anticipate the Divine compassion? Surely not with much degree of confidence.

If then they could gather but little hope of reprieve from the ministry of Jonah, *did they indulge it because they doubted the Divine Word ?* The Ninevites could

hardly doubt the fact that the Prophet had been
divinely commissioned to address them as he had done.
They must have known that he, a solitary man, would
not have undertaken so unthankful a duty unless
heaven had commanded it. The people would, therefore, necessarily associate him and his work with the
name and power of God. Then did they disbelieve
the threat of Jonah, and so continue in their sin?
Certainly not. We are emphatically told, in the narrative, that the Ninevites believed God, and that this
uplifting of their souls to Him was the first indication
of a better life. And in beautiful harmony with this
is the grief, deep and true, manifested by them, as
they seek the outflow of that love which was to
obliterate their past wickedness.

Then, if the Ninevites did not doubt the Divine
Word, *did they presume on the Divine mercy?* After a
careful reading of the narrative, we cannot even think
that they were guilty of this folly. If they believed
the Word of God, as we have seen they did, they certainly had not the faintest token of a future pardon.
Judgment, unmixed, was all they could expect, and
that not very far distant. Surely, then, under such
circumstances, the Ninevites would not risk their
safety to a forlorn hope, wildly dreaming that some
unknown power might come to their rescue. No, they
felt too much their position, the deep reality of their
sin, the terrible reproach of conscience, and the dire
force of circumstances around them, than to presume
on a phantom of their own imagination. What was it
then that caused the Ninevites to anticipate the forgiveness of God? *Did they not feel the enormity of*

their sin? Did they lightly estimate their national impurity as something not quite so woeful as Jonah had asserted? And that considering their comparative innocence, as compared with what they might have been, and as contrasted with the degeneracy of the people around them, such a punishment would be unjust, and was therefore unlikely to occur? No; the Ninevites did not reason thus. They admitted their wickedness, and, as the narrative shows, very deeply regretted it. Therefore we must look elsewhere for the explanation of this verse.

We believe that it was to be found *in that almost instinctive feeling of the human heart, that the Divine Being will deal with men according to their moral character.* The threat of impending doom was applied to Nineveh as sinful. Would not the promise of forgiveness be made to Nineveh as repentant? Of course, we must remember that we are in contact with heathen men and women, who would know nothing about the notions of popular theology as now received. But, deeper than these notions, in the human soul, is the thought that God will pardon the penitent, even though the first stern voice of woe may have announced destruction. By the prayer of grief, and faith in God, that voice may be turned into the glad hymn of peace, which shall lead the soul to repose more fully in its Saviour. Yes, men feel instinctively that God will not punish them for doing the right, and that though the past may have provoked His wrath, yet the dawning beauty of a new manhood will be likely to attract His pity, and will become a prayer for the renewal of His love. And God's love means the life of a penitent

nation, not its overthrow ; it means purity, not sin ;
hope, not despair ; and one ray of it from heaven is
almost enough to fill the world with gladness. Can we
wonder, then, when Nineveh, after her repentance,
became conscious of Divine mercy, that she exclaimed,
" Who can tell if God will turn and repent ? "

In the development of this hope within the heart of
Nineveh, *we behold the truest exercise of faith in God.*
It was no mere speculation that inspired and retained
this hope of pardon within the heart of Nineveh, notwithstanding the threat of Jonah, but it was a true
confidence in the Supreme Being, as Arbiter of the
moral destiny of men.   Only a fervent trust in God
can sustain the soul when it is seeking deliverance from
the judgment of sin.   In the development of this hope
we behold the first dawn of a new life.   Now the Ninevites are true to their better nature.   They are humble.
They are repentant.   They are working out in their
conduct the convictions placed in their hearts by the
Divine Spirit.   Their characters rise into new light,
and receive the beauty of a heavenly life.   In the
development of this hope *we behold a due recognition of
the anger of God.*   "And turn away from his fierce
anger that we perish not."   Had not the Ninevites
credited the Divine wrath, their faith would have been
untrue to fact, and their reformation of character would
not have been according to the circumstances of the
case.   In their change of character they believed in a
Deity capable of anger and destruction ; the former of
which they had truly excited, and the latter of which
they had but narrowly escaped. *But, notwithstanding the
hope that the Ninevites had in God, they were uncertain as*

to the result of the national humiliation, they said, "Who can tell if God will return." We must not presume too much on the power of our repentance and faith to stay the Divine wrath. But, having done our part, we must leave the result with that Being who is too wise to err and too good to be unkind.

And God saw their works, that they turned from their evil way ; and God repented of the evil, that he had said that he would do unto them ; and he did it not.—*Verse* 10.

In this verse we learn *the Divine observation of human repentance.* "And God saw their works, that they turned from their evil way." The Divine Being had been called to witness the sin of Nineveh, and it is now, with great joy, that His eye rests on her repentance. The transitions of moral character are minutely regarded by God, who is always glad to see the darkness of old manhood breaking into the beauty of the new. The first consciousness of sin, the first tear, speaking its silent language of grief, and the first prayer, tokens of a holier life, are earnestly watched by Him. In such matters as these society, in general, is but little interested ; it prefers something more tragical and exciting, more in harmony with its depraved inclinations. However, to God there is no sight more glorious than the first promise of better soul-life. And we are informed by Scripture that in this respect the angels are in truest sympathy with Him. "For likewise, I say unto you there is joy in the presence of the angels of God over one sinner that repenteth."* If

---

*Luke 15:10

then one penitent sinner is the occasion of celestial joy, what rapture would be inspired by the repentance of this vast multitude !

But this verse intimates not merely the Divine observation, *but also the Divine approval of the repentance of Nineveh.* God saw their works, approved them, and so averted the threatened punishment. We are not told that God remembered their fasting, or their sitting in sackcloth, or their prayers, but their turning away from their " evil way," as though this was the most pleasing and important feature in their humiliation. But when the narrative says that God saw their " works," it does not mean to indicate that His observation and approval extended merely to the externalisms of their late repentance, but more especially to the motive by which it had been prompted. All their outward observances, without the hidden power of faith, could never have gained the Divine commendation. Why then did this repentance of Nineveh so attract the favour of God ? *Because it was Divinely imparted.* The Ninevites did not beget this deep sorrow for sin in themselves by a vivid remembrance of the past, or by a doleful contemplation of the future. They may have thought much about their degeneracy, and the doom that was impending, as a consequence, but this alone would never have brought them to earnest prayer, and true reformation of character, unless a Divine influence had rested upon their hearts. True, Jonah aroused the heart of Nineveh by his preaching. True, the people observed a fast, and true the king and his nobles proclaimed it in the streets of the city, but behind all this there was an

unseen presence influencing the general consciousness of the multitude. And on this supposition only
can we account for the thoroughness of the repentance.

And thus, this national movement, being to a large
extent attributable to the powerful influence of the
Holy Spirit, was acceptable to God. Oh that in these
days we might be favoured with a like down-coming
of spiritual influence upon the heart of the world.
The repentance of the Ninevites was Divinely approved,
*because it would enhance the beauty and worth of their
moral character.* There is nothing by which man is
surrounded, capable of such transcendent beauty, as
moral character. The stars are very beautiful, shining
in the violet deeps of night. But their beauty is
unconscious, and they will one day lose their brightness. Flowers are lovely and fragrant, but they soon
decay ; whereas the splendour of moral character may,
by an earnest dependence upon God, be eternal, growing brighter and brighter unto the perfect day.* Its
beauty is conscious, and yet unconscious, however
paradoxical this may appear. The former in that it is
intelligent ; but the latter in that it is intensely modest.
And need we say that all this perfection is imparted
into our moral character by a penitent spirit, throwing
out its loveliness into every action, and transfusing our
life with a heavenly radiance. This repentance of the
Ninevites was Divinely approved, *because it would be
calculated to render happy their future destiny.* We
know the Supreme Being desires the eternal salvation
of the race. And anything tending to the accomplishment of this wins His commendation. We cannot tell

---

*Proverbs 4:18

whether this revival among the Ninevites was permanent
in its effects, or effervescent, like Ephraim's goodness.
No doubt the impression produced upon them by the
late events would give solemnity to their life for a time,
and then, perhaps, the danger gone, and the ministry
of Jonah almost forgotten, many would loose their
contrition of soul, and their enhanced worth of character
in the frivolity and progress of city life. But while
this might be the case with the general mass of the
people, there would yet remain a few noble spirits,
true to their renunciation of evil, and whose conduct
would anticipate a destiny much more happy than that
towards which they were previously tending. And
these would win the Divine approval as anticipated
additions to the ranks of heaven.

*Contemplate now the Divine conduct consequent upon
the repentance of Nineveh.* " And God repented of
the evil that he had said that he would do unto them ;
and he did it not." We need scarcely inform you that
the change of mind here predicated of the Divine
Being has given rise to much controversy, and attempted
explanation. One writer says, " Of course, it is after
the manner of men that the Spirit speaks, when He
attributes to God at any time repentance, or a change
of mind at all." * But this appears somewhat unsatis-
factory, as its tendency would be to divest God of all
true feeling and emotion. If we are not to understand
this language in reference to the Divine repentance as
literally true, what will become of all those passages
that announce to us the love of God. For if one is
after " the manner of men," the other must be, which

---

*Rev. H. Martin, M.A., *The Prophet Jonah*, page 373.

we should be sorry to admit. This explanation appears
little better than a subterfuge to get out of the difficulty, and, in our opinion, does but increase it. Another
writer says, in reference to this passage, " This was no
real change in God; rather, the object of His threatening
was, that He might not do what He threatened. God's
threatenings are conditional, ' unless they repent,' as
are His promises, ' if they endure to the end." God
says afterwards by Jeremiah,* " at that instant I shall
speak concerning a kingdom, to pluck up and to pull
down and to destroy it, if that nation, against whom I
had pronounced, turn from their evil, I will repent of
the evil that I thought to do unto them." † Another
writer says, "As God is unchangeable in nature, so is
He unchangeable in will; for no one can turn back His
thoughts. For, though some seem to have turned
back His thoughts by their deprecations, yet this was
His inward thought, that they should be able by their
deprecations to turn back His sentence, and that they
should receive from Him whereby to avail with Him.
When, then, outwardly His sentence seemeth to be
changed; inwardly, His counsel is unchanged, because
He inwardly ordereth each thing unchangeably, what-
soever is done outwardly with change." ‡ It would
then seem from this, that in making a threat, the
Divine Being has " an inward counsel " and " an outward sentence," and that while the latter may change,
the former cannot. True, this is an ingenious attempt
to unfold the difficulty, but does it not seem complex

---

*Jeremiah 18:7-8   †Dr. Pusey on *Minor Prophets.*
‡St. Gregory quoted by Dr. Pusey in his *Commentary on the Minor
Prophets.*

and inadequate. For whether we designate the threat itself "an outward sentence" or "an inward counsel," there can be no doubt that when God announced the overthrow of Nineveh He meant it inwardly, or He could not have meant it at all. Then, if He was turned from this determination by the repentance of Nineveh, may He not be said to have repented inwardly; and we contend that, in so doing, He acted in harmony with the truest principle of His government, and, also, for the best welfare of man. However, we cannot disguise the fact that this threat, though meant, was conditional, or else the Ninevites could not have expected, by their prayers, to have averted it. Then, if the Divine Being knew that they would comply with this condition, why did He threaten them with destruction? Because this threat, and the crisis it would occasion, were the means of their reformation; but for which the Ninevites would not have been awakened to a consciousness of their sin. They all felt that their threatened overthrow was just, hence their humiliation. Why should it be thought incredible that God "repents" or "changes?" Would it not be more incredible if it were asserted that He never does? Would it be to the honor of God if it could be said with truth that He thinks and feels concerning us *in one condition*, exactly as He would if we were in a condition the very opposite? Among men, a good father, a just master, will treat a son or servant according to their works and their state. When they wickedly transgress he is grieved and and angry. When they repent and reform he is glad and pleased. Such a man is not called fickle and changeable in nature on account of these changing states. Because he has integrity, and love in his nature has unchanging principles; therefore, as the ever-varying facts and scenes of life arise and pass before him, as the different acts and moral states of men are perceived, there are emotions corresponding with them excited in his mind. And are we to suppose that what constitutes a special perfection in the moral character of a man is an imperfection in God? Surely not." * Thus we cannot for a moment connect this repentance of God with any thought of weakness; on the contrary, it is a proof of the immutable principles by which He is actuated. And, in this case, His conduct was most merciful, saving thousands of lives, together with all the interests of a vast city, And, in this, we cannot but see the glory of that God whose nature and property is ever to have mercy and to forgive.

Lastly, we learn from this verse *the utility of a national humiliation.* It is well for a people when they have, in Supreme authority, men who are disposed to recognise the corrective Providence of God. For we know not how much misery and sin might be averted by an occasional day of humiliation and prayer. And if on such an occasion our aristocracy, instead of going in state and pageantry to St. Paul's, would follow more the example of the king and nobles of Nineveh, in the simplicity of their conduct and thoroughness of their grief, we doubt not that the humiliation would be more effective and acceptable to the Divine Being.

We have now come to the conclusion of this third chapter; in it we have seen blended, in the history of

---

*Alexander Raleigh, *The Story of Jonah*, page 250.

a vast people, the anger and mercy of God, the latter ultimately breaking forth upon the page to the entire removal of the former. We have heard the prayers, and seen the reformed character of a heathen nation. Also we have witnessed the great power of one life to influence a city for good. Why should a man who could work like this have refused to undertake the mission to Nineveh? We know not the true capacity of our soul for work until it is tried by circumstances; and many there are who might be erecting great spiritual temples in Nineveh, drudges in Tarshish, because they will not, in obedience to the Divine command, go to the sphere, and undertake the duty confided to their care.

We cannot, however, conclude our exposition of this chapter without making one or two general remarks. *If Nineveh repented under such a ministry, and in so short a time, what will be our condemnation, if found finally impenitent at the bar of God?* This is a very solemn question, and demands an immediate reply. We have not had an unwilling Jonah sent to make known our sin, but a compassionate and ever willing Jesus. Not merely one prophet has been sent to threaten us, but a thousand. Nor have the messages addressed to us been all stern and dark, but kind and loving; they have appealed to the tenderest sympathies of our truer nature. And instead of being privileged with such ministries as these for *one day*, you have had them for years. What the better are you for them to-day; nay, are you not morally the worse, because you have resisted their constant and pathetic appeals. Your heart is hardened; oh, terrible is the issue and the condemnation brought upon the soul by these neglects. " Verily the men of Nineveh shall rise up in judgment with this generation, and shall condemn it; for they repented at the preaching of Jonas; and, behold, a greater than Jonas is here."* And not only will the men of Nineveh rise up to condemn us, but the cannibals of Fiji, the myriads of India, and the vast tribes of South Africa, and before these men, whose lives were blessed with but few ministries to awaken their thought, instruct their mind, quicken their conscience, and arouse their spiritual feeling, we, of this Christian Isle, so richly favoured with all the choicest benedictions of heaven, shall stand confused and ashamed to acknowledge their moral superiority.

Who can sound the depths unknown,
    Of Thy redeeming grace ?
Grace, that gave Thine only Son
    To save a ruined race.
Millions of transgressors poor,
    Thou hast for Jesu's sake forgiven :
Made them of thy favour sure,
    And snatched from hell to heaven.

Millions more Thou ready art
    To save, and to forgive ;
Every soul and every heart
    Of man Thou would'st receive.
Father, now accept of mine,
    Which now, through Christ, I offer Thee.
Tell me now, in love divine,
    That Thou hast pardoned me !

_____

*Luke 11:32.

JONAH 4

WE now come to the last scene in this remarkable drama, and, in many respects, a very different one from any before contemplated. It would appear almost as if Jonah had now undergone a moral transformation, for instead of beholding an earnest preacher, we see a weak-tempered mortal, under the corrective discipline of God. He is no longer engaged in contrite devotion, as in the second chapter; in fact, he is more like the Prophet of the first chapter, quarrelling with the Divine Providence. This change is pitiable and sad to behold. We had thought Jonah to be an entirely new man; that his fall had imparted altogether a new condition of moral worth to his character. But here we have a token that there yet remains in his manhood a something that impairs its vigour and mars its beauty. It would have been better for the Prophet had the curtain fallen upon him while in the attitude of devotion, or while he was preaching to the doomed crowds in the streets of Nineveh. We almost feel as if he had lived too long for the good of his reputation; as if it would have been better had his life closed with the third chapter, leaving the fourth unenacted and unwritten. However, let the picture here given, of a petulant spirit, deter us from ever cherishing a like temper, whatever may be the varied circumstances of our lives. We see in this narrative the strict integrity of the Sacred writers, in that they do not endeavour to conceal their faults, but honestly make their real characters the pedestal of heavenly light, by the aid of which men can find their way to the true secret of life and glory.

But it displeased Jonah exceedingly, and he was very angry.— *Verse* 1.

The subject of this verse is *a Petulant Man*. Jonah had now very nearly completed his mission to Nineveh. He had preached against the city, and had aroused it to a state of penitent reflection. In fact, we might almost say that he had done his work wisely and well, and that it was likely to be productive of the most happy result. He found the nation joining in one song of revelry ; he has left it in the holy attitude of prayer. And God, seeing the changed condition of its life, is about to remove the threatened curse by the glad prediction of His mercy. No longer is Nineveh to be encircled by the fires of Divine anger, but she is to enter into rich experiences of the Divine compassion. Instead of overthrow, there is to be established in her midst a new temple of living souls, pure and holy, for the abode of God. Instead of confusion, there is to be order; instead of disfigurement, there is to be beauty, and instead of ruin, there is to be progress. In short, a truer moral grandeur will rest on the city than ever known before; for the renewed manhood will impart the glory of its inner spirit to all around. The mercy of God will be written on every stone in Nineveh, as well as on every human heart. How

great then will be the joy of the Prophet that his
ministry is thus connected with a change of life so
happy, with a purpose so unspeakably grand as the
salvation of so vast a crowd.

Had the narrative been silent as to the manner in
which Jonah received the tidings of Nineveh's reprieve,
we should have imagined him in an ecstacy of spirit ;
as rejoicing in a hymn of praise. But how widely such
fancies would have been from the truth the inspired
record shews, for instead of ecstacy, there was despair ;
instead of joy, there was sorrow ; and instead of lauding
the mercy of God, *the Prophet was lamenting a fancied
injustice done to his prophetic reputation.* Do we find a
counterpart to this picture to-day ? Are there any
ministers now who think more about their popularity,
than about the eternal welfare of those around them ?
Oh, terrible thought. Is it possible that any minister
of Christ can be found who would for a moment hold
his fancied reputation as of more importance than the
salvation of a city ; than even the good of one soul,
that has to think and live for ever ? No ! let us be
more self-forgetful. Mere reputation at best is but a
fickle light, which a gush of unkindly breath may
extinguish. Our great aim should be to secure reputation in the heavenly city, as the most successful soul-
winner on earth ! This honour might have belonged to
Jonah, but he lost sight of its quiet lustre, in his
desire for the lurid grandeur of an earthly fame.

We gather from all this that *a petulant man is out
of sympathy with the grand purposes of God.* The
Divine purpose in reference to Nineveh was most merciful ; the city was to be saved from ruin, and its inhabi-

tants from death. It is this consideration that excites
our wonder at the petulance of Jonah, for it is
certainly far more natural for man, and especially a
good man, to sympathise with the safety of a people,
than with their destruction. God wished that Nineveh
should enter upon an entirely new moral history,
every page of which should shine resplendent with His
love. Nineveh was to be saved · from the tramp
of invading armies, from the immediate stroke of God.
She was to be joyous, and purity was to be the altar
at which her gladness should be kindled. Yea, her
new life was to be crowned with all the choicest blessings of heaven. Yet, strange to say, when Jonah
becomes aware of this, he at once gives way to selfish
temper, and unthankful speech. Nor does he confine
these to himself, allowing them merely to reign within
the narrow circle of his own heart, but brings them
into the very presence of God, and embodies them in
prayer. And so it is with petulant men. They are
out of sympathy with the merciful plans of God. Any
providence that seems to thwart their caprice, to impair
their dignity, to lessen their fame, or the apparent
value of their service, they at once condemn, even
though it contemplates the eternal welfare of a once
doomed city. How un-prophet like is such conduct,
and how unworthy of a man like Jonah, who ought to
have immediately responded to the wish of God.

Further, *a petulant man is out of sympathy with the
highest good of those around him.* God, in response to
the prayer of Nineveh, was about to countermand the
overthrow He had threatened. Yet this is the occasion of
Jonah's petulance. We have seen that he was more

anxious for his own repute, as a Prophet, than for the good of his fellow-creatures, as though it would be more honourable for his name to be associated with the destruction, than the salvation of Nineveh. He, probably, thought that only in the former case would it be associated with that of the Divine Being, as though it was not so God-like to forgive Nineveh as to cause its destruction. But Jonah looked more at the words of his message than at their inner spirit; he thought more of the rough externalism of his duty than of its underlying sentiment of compassion. The life of Nineveh was to be continued. The soul of Nineveh was to be elevated from its degradation to purity and peace. Men were to be in sympathy one with the other. Families were to enter into a truer and Diviner meaning of the word home, than ever before experienced. The national institutions were not to be the mere shadows of power and truth, but the reality of all that was regal and noble. The people were to live in an almost ideal commonwealth. And yet, with all this great good to Nineveh, Jonah was out of sympathy.

 Again, *a petulant man is out of sympathy with the mercy of God, as experienced in his own history*. Had not Jonah, only a little while ago, been in the same position as the Ninevites are now? Yea, had not the punishment of disobedience overtaken him? Had he not been cast into the sea, and confined within the precincts of a great fish? Then, the sailors, with whom he voyaged, did not manifest a petulant spirit, not even when they discovered him to be the secret of their peril, but rowed hard to bring him to land. And, not

only had man shewn him sympathy in his danger, but
also God. For, while in the belly of the fish his life
was preserved, and ultimately, in a miraculous way,
delivered from its sentence of imprisonment. Surely,
then, here was a discipline that ought to have prepared
Jonah for the exigencies of the present moment.
A remembrance of his own history ought to have
inspired him with sympathy towards the repentance of
Nineveh. But no! he is animated by a petulant
spirit, which renders him insensible to the instruction
of his past life.

*How morally degrading to the character of Jonah is
this petulant spirit.* This is partly evinced by the pre-
ceding consideration; for, if a man is out of sympathy
with the Divine purpose, with the moral good of his
fellows, and with the merciful experiences of his past
life, his position cannot be very dignified. Nor can the
temper which causes this disunion be praiseworthy.
On the other hand, it is a great evidence of moral
weakness, and we almost wonder that it should be found
in a manhood like that of Jonah's. Petulance is a
most unworthy temper of the soul, both in the sight of
God and man.

This narrative shews us *that great men have often
some weak side to their characters,* otherwise we might
be tempted to worship them. It very often happens
that men who have performed some great service, which
the world will never forget, are shortly afterwards found
to be the victim of some, so-called, little weakness.
Great natures have to be on their guard against petulant tempers. A giant was slain by a small pebble, so
a Jonah may be enfeebled by a peevish disposition.

These transitory manifestations of temper have a much more permanent influence upon our character than we are inclined to admit. How much more noble would it have been on the part of Jonah had he rejoiced in the reprieve of Nineveh, and so have been in harmony with the kindly providence of God. He would then have appeared unselfish and calm, capable of the two extremes of service, that of hard toil, and also that of self-conquest; whereas, now he is presented to us as a man who could preach to, and move a large city, but who could not exercise self-control. It was easier for Jonah to conquer Nineveh, than himself. It would seem as though he had not altogether recovered from his first fall, so thoroughly does this display of temper dim the brightness of his renewed character. Thus we see the weakness, degradation, and suspicion that a petulant temper brings even upon a Prophet. Such a temper is unworthy of a Christian worker.

Lastly, *we see how miserable petulance makes a man*. Jonah had finished his mission, the hardships connected therewith were at an end, and, for ought we know, he might have wended his way home in peace; but, instead of this, we find him on a foreign shore, a desolate and angry man. It is impossible for a petulant spirit to be happy, even though all else around is cheering. The fancied wrong is more powerful to disquiet, than all the memories of a successful mission in Nineveh to calm. It makes men take a partial view of life. It fills the scene with a moodiness by no means pleasant. The petulant man is an object of pity. He might be happy, but will not. He is his own worst enemy, alienating himself from every source of com-

fort. Let his portrait, as given in this chapter, keep us
from ever imitating his spirit, lest it bring a like unrest
upon our lives.

And he prayed unto the Lord, and said, I pray thee, O Lord,
was not this my saying, when I was yet in my country? Therefore
I fled before unto Tarshish: for I knew that thou art a gracious
God, and merciful, slow to anger, and of great kindness, and
repentest thee of the evil.—*Verse 2.*

In this verse we have *a man praying in a petulant
spirit.* It is evident that Jonah has not lost all his
religion yet, but is simply impatient, and vexed at the
manifestation of Divine mercy to Nineveh. Though
distracting thoughts are passing through his mind, and
unpeaceful feelings agitating his soul, he still prays to
that God who had so recently delivered him from
trouble. We can imagine circumstances in which it is
a good thing for an angry man to pray. Though, at
first, unfit for the solemn exercise, yet as he waits at
the footstool of heaven, a holy calm comes upon his
nature, new hopes are awakened within him, and instead
of the strife of a rebellious will, there is ultimately the
peace of a soul in harmony with that of the great
Parent of the universe. If men who are sometimes
thwarted in the plans of life, who find things going
contrary to their wish, and who feel as though their
ideas of right were violated, would check the first
impulse to passion, the first voice of murmuring, by the
importunity of devotion, many a sad and terrible
deed would remain unacted. It seems a wonder that
Jonah's petulance lasted so long as it seems to have
done, and that it was not quickly removed by the

fervour of prayer, but required the special and continued discipline of God. He does not appear to
realize the benefit of devotion that men generally do.
And why ? Because his anger was too persistent to
yield its argument even at the throne of grace. Jonah
did not pray that God would help him to overcome his
temper, but urged his request under its unholy influence.
He manifested no desire to overcome it. He was contented that it should reign within him. Yea, perhaps,
he thought it was a righteous indignation after the
supposed injury he had suffered. It is useless for men
to pray in anger unless they seek to overcome it, otherwise it is little better than mockery.

We see that Jonah, praying in this petulant spirit,
attempts to vindicate his past misconduct. " O Lord,
was not this my saying when I was yet in my country ?
Therefore I fled before unto Tarshish." What a common picture is this. Men are ever willing to vindicate
their past unfaithfulness. And, even when they have
passed into higher and better experiences, they are
glad to make the unfoldings of everyday life lend some
pencillings of light to the dark picture of the past.
Jonah tells the Divine Being that but for the thought
of Divine mercy he should have obeyed the first command to Nineveh. And thus he tries to make his new
circumstances justify his old sins. But how was it that
the Prophet did not think of this excuse before ? Why
did he not name it to the sailors as a reason why they
should not cast him into the sea ? Why did he not
mention it in his prayer of the second chapter, as an
argument why God should release him from the belly
of the great fish. He did not attempt to palliate his

disobedience there, probably it would not have fared so well with him if he had. The truth is that his new experiences of the Divine love are a temptation to him, and presented in a light favourable to his past career, he embodies their suggestion in this prayer. He thought the plea was forceful; and, certainly, it sounded well. But it was the utterance of a man attempting a vain impossibility, to justify that condemned by every holy instinct of his nature. How Satan can delude men thus to invest the new-born thought of to-day with the age of years, so that it may stand, with some degree of authority, to defend a wicked past. Let us never try to excuse past disobedience, it is unworthy of it, it is best left in the depths of that oblivion into which the Divine Being consigns our forgiven transgressions. As we contemplate the spirit and argument of this verse, we are given to feel that long shadows are growing over the brightness of Jonah's repentant character, that will need to be chased away again by the mercy of God. For the truest element of repentance is a consciousness of having done a wrong no plea can excuse.

Further, we find that Jonah, praying in this spirit, *appears to reproach the character of God.* "For I knew that thou art a gracious God, and merciful, slow to anger, and of great kindness, and repentest thee of the evil." Perhaps some of you may wonder that we should consider such a glorious description reproachful to the Divine character. True, if it stood alone it could not be so regarded, as it would be true as it is beautiful, and consoling in the experiences of life. But the reflection on the Divine character is more implied than expressed, and may not have been directly intended by the Prophet. Jonah intimates that God was so merciful that He was not just, and that He would not execute judgment against the wicked. The language is expressive of weakness in the Divine character. For if this verse is true, that God will not punish such cities as Nineveh, so degraded by evil, because of His natural leniency, then farewell to the possibility of religious service. There will be wicked cities, but it will be vain for us to go to foretell their doom. But the argument of Jonah was founded on a wrong supposition. True, God is merciful, but He is also just, and though He will save a nation, under certain conditions of moral life, He can nevertheless rain fire and brimstone upon it if impenitent. The Divine requirement is that men do their duty, as commanded by "the word of the Lord." And Prophets doing this, will always find their service sustained by the character of God.

This narrative shews us *how very important it is, for a right performance of the practical service of life, that we should have right views of the Divine character.* If we have not correct notions of God, our lives are sure to be feeble, and we are in danger of inconceivable woe. All worthy religious service and effort must be founded on a right apprehension of the Divine nature. And it is only when the mystery of the Divine life is seen in the incarnate Person of Christ, as inviolably holy, and inflexibly just, that human life has a sure basis for its action, and a true guide for its otherwise perilous journeyings.

Therefore now, O Lord, take, I beseech thee, my life from me; for it is better for me to die than to live.— *Verse 3.*

In this verse we see *what imaginary trouble a petulant spirit brings upon a man*. Because the Divine Being was determined to save Nineveh, here is Jonah praying that an end may be made to his life. He would rather loose his life than his fancied reputation as a Prophet, hence he cries for the grave to hide him from the expected satire of the world. Jonah thought that his mission to Nineveh was a failure, when in reality the late out-working of events proved it to have been a grand success. And the truest element of the success was the mercy that God had caused to shine upon that otherwise dark city. But the Prophet's petulant temper rendered him insensible to this glorious manifestation of heavenly approval. And even his fellow-creatures would have applauded an end so noble. Jonah's troubles were entirely imaginary. They were the dark phantoms of his own fancy, flitting through his soul, which a calm glimpse into the purpose of God, in reference to the eternal destiny of Nineveh, would have dispelled. And how many men, especially those who work for the public good, are haunted by troubles as unreal as were those of Jonah. They imagine that all goes wrong with them, and even when their spiritual success is greatest, allow some little thought of self to alloy its pleasure. Half the sorrows of life are the mere fancies of a peevish temper. We permit harsh thoughts of God to reign within our souls. We think that the interests of our little name are of more importance than the destiny of a great city, and go into airs of impatience if the former are

made subservient to the latter. Here is the secret of
pain. If we could only get rid of the selfish tempers
that often sweep athwart our souls, half the depressing
influences of life would be gone, and the scene of this
verse would be known only as an exception.

What a depressing effect have imaginary troubles
upon a human life. *Imaginary troubles make men think
that their power of work is exhausted.* Jonah had done
his work in Nineveh well. He had made one supreme
effort to achieve his God-given task. And now comes
the reaction consequent upon the energy that had been
called into exercise during the past few days, especially
as things have turned out contrary to his wish. He
therefore feels as if his moral nature were exhausted,
as if all his power of effort were gone ; and his highest
hope is to die at once. He seems as if all motive had
passed from his soul, as if a dark gloom had settled
upon his life, and he lay passively under its shadow.
Nor is this picture an uncommon one. Many men
who have put all their energies into one great enterprise, upon finding it going contrary to their hope,
have been so depressed as to loose all the activities of
their nature. They have appeared as though the
memories of the past prevented the out-coming of new
energy and new hope. A petulant spirit renders men
unfit for spiritual work.

*They make men think that they can be no longer useful
to their fellows.* They feel as though they themselves
had not the force of character to go to Nineveh again ;
and, even if they were to make a determined effort
and attain it, that the inhabitants would slight their
prophetic rank. The Prophets think that those to

whom they preached might point to the past prediction,
and shew that, instead of the threatened overthrow,
there was the exhibition of mercy. They think that
this might render the people sceptical to their future
denunciation. And no doubt there would be some
who might presume upon this reprieve of Nineveh,
that the mercy manifested to her at the last hour,
would also be extended to them. But the Prophet's
earnestness would soon rise above this momentary
hindrance, and impress the people with the reality of
his mission. But we think that, after all, a Prophet
who went to another mission, armed with the authority
given him by the repentance and reprieve of Nineveh,
would have far greater likelihood of success, than
if he had been associated with the ruin of so vast
a city. In the former case he would be associated
with the power of love, with the charm of mercy,
with the sympathy of benevolent effort, with the
beauty of a kindly spirit; whereas, in the latter case,
he would be associated with retribution and woe. And
we know to which argument the human soul is most
sensitive, even though the love manifested may involve,
to those who have not vision into the mysteries of God,
an apparent contradiction. Had Jonah gone to another
mission over the scattered ruins of Nineveh, the people
would have looked upon him as a dark herald of woe,
they would have been frightened at him, they would
have avoided him, and have closed their ears to his
every cry, lest it should be an announcement of wrath;
but, going with the tidings of Nineveh's reprieve
and moral beauty, the crowd would gather round,
and welcome him to their sympathy and homes.

But Jonah, under the influence of a peevish temper, could not see the advantage of the present arrangement of things, and so thinking that his day of usefulness was over, cried out for death. And a like spirit has equally deprossed men of our own day, they have thought themselves altogether incapable of good to their fellow-creatures, and hence have wished to die.

Imaginary troubles make men think *that death will be a welcome relief to their grief.* Jonah prayed that he might die. Elijah had uttered the same prayer before him. It is a prayer that only a man of a great nature could present in sincerity. Only a Prophet of great soul could be capable of such an effort, as to occasion the exhaustion and grief indicated by it. The prayer is an index to the great struggle that had gone before it. Only a man who could preach alone to the impenitent crowds of Nineveh could utter it. Only a man who could confront the thousands of heathendom on Carmel could articulate it. This prayer is the unbending of a soul so prostrated by effort that it could only long for death. It is extremely painful for such men to be çonscious of moral weakness, and yet such a consciousness is the only balance to their strength. But death would not have given Jonah the relief he wanted, for instead of removing him from all thought of, and responsibility in respect to Nineveh, it would have brought him into the presence of Him with whose Providence he was in conflict, and whose mercy he was anxious to avert from the perishing multitude. Death is not extinction. If it were, the grave would hush the world's cry of sorrow, and give to the vexed Prophet rest from the annoyances

of life.   No! death is continued being, and that
under conditions, which render it more solemn and
intense.   Hence death would only have led Jonah
from the shadow of his trouble to its very centre,
where its sad meaning would have been made known to
him.   The same man who had been associated with
the mission to Nineveh on earth, in the next world
would have found himself in the same moral relationship, in unhappy remembrance of his petulant temper.   Hence death would have been little advantage
to him, for had it shielded him from the reproach of
men, it would have opened him to the judgment of
God.

*What a mercy it is that God does not always respond
to the unthinking prayers of men under the influence of
trouble, caused by unholy temper.*   God had shewn
the same mercy to Jonah, as he now manifests to the
Ninevites.   When Jonah prayed to be delivered from
the belly of the great fish God heard him, because that
was for his personal good; but now that he prays
for violence and injury to his soul and body, God merci-
fully refuses to comply with his request.   The Divine
Being is discreet in answering our prayers.   God saw
that Jonah was under the influence of a petulant
temper.   He knew that he did not see things in their
real bearing, and so compassionated his grief by the
gentle chiding of these verses.   What woe would be
brought upon our lives if God were to give all we prayed
for.   It is a mercy that the Divine Being does not respond
to all the unthinking supplications of the human heart.

Then said the Lord, doest thou well to be angry?—*Verse* 4.

Now God again joins Himself to the Prophet's life. And as He had striven to correct his disobedience by confinement in the mighty deep, He now endeavours to reason Jonah out of his petulant temper. The Divine Being does not always like to use extreme penalties, but the more gentle, that men may not only be disciplined by pain, but also by moral conviction. Hence God frequently comes to the human soul in the language of this verse, and says, "Doest thou well to be angry." And this quiet method of correction is frequently effective, awaking in the soul thoughts that end in a return to reason and purity. It would seem, however, that the discipline of argument was not sufficient to bring Jonah to an acknowledgment of his wrong temper; hence a practical illustration, materially affecting his comfort was appended. When the Divine Being has laid down an argument, He is never at a loss for a suitable illustration whereby to enforce its teaching.

It is an evidence of great condescension on the part of God in that He will to reason with men under such conditions of moral life. This is not the first time that Jonah has manifested a dislike to the Divine purpose, and therefore we could not have been surprised if God had brought sudden destruction upon him, without one indication of its approach. If we consider the present appeal in the light of Jonah's past conduct, it gathers new meaning, and is resplendent with unexampled forbearance. The Prophet had wished for the destruction of Nineveh, had striven to vindicate his past dis-

obedience ; had made false insinuations in reference to
the Divine character, and had embodied the desire of an
evil temper in prayer. Yet this is the man with whom
God condescends to reason. Not an honest sceptic,
who, not knowing the truth, is sincerely asking Divine
guidance; not a man who, alternating between faith
and doubt, is waiting for more evidence to establish
him in the former. But with a man who has a second
time brought himself into antagonism with the Infinite.
The Divine Being tries to reason Jonah out of his sin ;
this is just what He is attempting with every one of
us. Nor does our past life, marked as it has been by
evil of every kind, deter Him from the expostulation.
He addresses our souls in a voice not to be mistaken,
" doest thou well to be angry." If God can only get
men to view their sins in the light of reason, with calm
spirit, it will be the first step toward a new and brighter
life. The truest goodness is always the highest reason.

The folly of an angry spirit is seen *in that it cannot
change the circumstances that have aroused it.* The
anger of Jonah was called forth by the Divine determination to save the people of Nineveh. Nor could
the anger of the Prophet avert this glad reprieve. We
see, as a matter of fact, that it did not. God had more
regard for the great city than to yield up its eternal
welfare to the peevish cry of a disappointed man. No,
Jonah's temper could not alter the circumstances of
the case in the slightest degree, but only made them
the channel of more terrible agony to himself. If men,
who are given to such manifestations of anger, would
only consider that they cannot govern their surroundings
by the rod of passion, how soon would they lay it

down.   If we would control our circumstances, prayer
to heaven, and trust in God only, can put into our
hands a sceptre that shall enable us to do so calmly.
Jonah lacked this supreme confidence in God, and hence
was thrown into disquiet and anger.

The folly of an angry temper is seen *in that it cannot
give quietude under the trials that have called it forth.*
Does Jonah stand before us now in tranquil spirit?
Certainly not.   We have never before seen him in such
a condition of unrest.   He was far more calm when
the sailors were going to cast him into the sea.   He
was far more peaceful when praying in the belly of
the great fish.   And why?   The only reply we can
give is, that because under these trials he retained
power over his temper.   And, as a matter of happiness,
a man had far better be in circumstances of peril with
a prayerful spirit, than in the height of achievement with a petulant temper.   I doubt not that the
Prophet felt a truer repose of soul in the belly of
the great fish than in his sublime conquest over
Nineveh, and in the experiences of this chapter.   A bad
temper has a terrible power to bring disquietude upon
a life.   If you wish to render yourself and all around
you miserable, you can soon do so by giving way to
the disposition now manifested by Jonah.   There are
multitudes of men whose only grief is a petulant
spirit, and if this were removed, they would look out
upon life with new joy, and all the dark phantoms that
now fill their lives with fear, would be turned into
angels, to fill them with hope.   A petulant temper will
put the world in mourning, will turn every marriage
party into a funeral procession, and every merry child

into a mocking satire.   Whereas, a kindly disposition
will make the universe radiant with beauty and vocal
with song.   Which temper do you cultivate?   Let
your daily companion reply.

Then the folly of an angry temper is seen *in that
it only prompts men to a display of moral weakness.*
Has Jonah ever appeared so morally little as he does
now?   He seems more like a child than a man; more
like a timid believer than a stalwart Prophet.   We
look at him preaching in Nineveh, and feel that the
man reaches to the full measure of his office and work.
We see him now, but are inclined to pass a very
different judgment upon him. Men never appear so small
in the eyes of their fellows as when under the influence
of a petulant spirit.   Then it is that they seem unfit
for extreme effort, while, in reality, they may have just
accomplished marvellous success.   So completely may
this disposition divest a great man of the glory of his
past achievement.   It renders him a contradiction to
himself, and a sport to all around him.   Many a truly
great man holds but trivial place in public esteem,
simply because he has occasionally manifested petulant
airs, which have rendered him a by-word to, rather than
a leader of the people.   They do not get their due,
but they have only themselves to blame for it.   It is a
pity that men of such great qualities should cause
themselves thus to be undervalued; that they should
be deprived of their social and moral standing by such
petty displays of temper.   Let us try to rise into such
a calmness of soul, resulting from continued faith in
God, that all the troublous events of life may find us
ready to meet them with open hand and winning smile.

Then our moral disposition will blend in lovely harmony with the great powers of our nature, by which we won the victory in Nineveh. Then the world will admire our moral self-consistency, and be willing to help us in all our efforts of progress.

The folly of an angry temper is seen *in that it excites the displeasure of God*. While in God's dealings with Jonah, as recorded in these verses, there is an outbeaming of mercy; there is, nevertheless, a background of punishment. There is in this discipline an indication of judgment. True, God reasons with the Prophet, but the argument is such as to manifest his folly. True, God prepared him a gourd, but He also prepared a worm for its destruction; hence there is in the narrative an interplay of Divine love and displeasure manifested towards the Prophet. We should ever remember that all our angry dispositions are calculated to excite the Divine displeasure; especially when they are occasioned in us by the merciful providences of heaven towards penitent sinners. We should not contend with the Infinite. How impotent does the anger of Jonah appear; its greatest effort was as nothing in comparison with the Divine operation in reference thereto. Anger leads men into presumption, and that sometimes in the most solemn sphere of their lives. In a moment Jonah might have been hurried into eternity, there to meet the awful responsibilities of his anger. But God is merciful even to men in their weakness. Let the picture of these few verses teach you resignation amid the disturbing events of every day life, that your spirit, instead of being angry, may be prayerful, and instead of being unpeaceful, may be calm.

So Jonah went out of the city, and sat on the east side of the city, and there made him a booth, and sat under it in the shadow, till he might see what would become of the city.—*Verse 5.*

In this verse we have *a man waiting to see the final issue of his religious work.* There are times in the life of every religious worker when it is well for him to pause, and review the nature and value of bygone service. Men who toil continuously, without reflection, are likely, very soon, to pursue a wrong course of action, or, at least, to enfeeble their energies by the want of repose. And especially, at certain periods of effort, is a waiting attitude of soul most fitting; at the end of one mission, or the commencement of another, we cannot do better than spend an hour with self and God.

We see that *Jonah waited away from the scene of his past labours.* "So Jonah went out of the city." If Nineveh is to be overthrown, he departs that he may not share her ruin; if not, that he may escape the odium of a false prophet. "And sat on the east side of the city." Perhaps, in this direction, there was a hill from which he could survey the crowds of Nineveh; or, as the river Tigris ran on the west side, he may have gone eastward to avoid the travellers to its haven. Many people, in these days, take a great delight in turning toward the east, especially when they recite the Apostle's Creed, as though the Divine Presence were more in that direction than in any other. Certain it is that Jonah was not animated by any such fancy in the selection of his eastward course. There can be little doubt that *his great purpose was to gain solitude.* And in this desire we apprehend that Jonah was right; for when the worker for the spiritual welfare of men is wishful to review the past, he cannot do better than leave the scene of his activity, and retire into solitude, that away from all that would attract his attention, or excite his pity, he may the more thoroughly reflect on its success or otherwise. For there in quietude, alone with God, he will the more deeply realize the personal responsibility of his work, he will find more unerringly the secret of past failure, and gain enhanced ability for future duty. The great preacher cannot always remain in the densely crowded city. He must come forth for recreation, as well as for spiritual invigoration. The eastward walk is equally beneficial to the moral, as the physical nature, of the true preacher. But the retirement of Jonah from activity to rest, from the crowd to loneliness, was not helpful either to his body or his soul, because he carried with him an angry spirit, which peopled his solitude with imaginary sorrows, by no means welcome to an exhausted worker.

We find that *during his waiting he was not unmindful of his personal comfort.* " And there made him a booth." He probably cut down a few boughs, and made a kind of hut, under the shadow of which he could repose. Nor do we find fault with him for this. His conduct was perfectly natural and wise. The servants of God do not always find necessary preparations made for their comfort in this world ; they are often alone, destitute of home, outside the great city. It is well for them, at such times, if they have an inventive genius, and can make a booth for themselves, in the absence of anything better. Preachers should never be above making their own booths ; they will probably be as well made by themselves as by anyone else. A bad temper has given many a man reason to make a booth to shelter him since the days of Jonah. But while we can in no way blame the Prophet for looking after his temporal comfort, yet he is certainly culpable in neglecting the higher duties that should have occupied his attention during these important moments of quietude. If he felt the necessity of making a booth during his suspense, he ought far more thoroughly to have acknowledged the need of self-communion, of prayer to God, and of true resignation to the Divine will. Whereas now, the comfort afforded by the booth does but indicate his neglect, in that he made no precaution to shade his *soul* from the fierce rays, of an impending judgment. This is a true picture of life to-day. Multitudes of men are far more anxious about their booths than their souls. How pitiful that such should be the case, and especially amongst the prophetic order.

We find that *Jonah awaited the issue of his Nineveh service in idleness.* He sat in indolence under the shadow of his booth, fretfully awaiting the outworking of the future in reference to the city. He did not think of the sin and repentance of the people to whom he had preached. He did not wait in prayer the final issue of his toil. His eye, instead of being turned upward toward God, or inward upon self, was all the while watching the crowds of Nineveh, and their changing attitudes of character in relation to his prophetic reputation. He spends this interval of service in angry, unthankful mood, incapable of effort. When we retire from active duty to review its worth and await its issue, let us be careful not to idle our time away. After the

fatigue of service we shall be tempted to undue repose,
but solitude is too rare and divine a thing to be made
the scene of indolence, especially when the zeal of the
preacher should be followed by the earnest waiting of the
saint.   At such a time the most active energies of our
spirit should be awakened.   We should prayerfully re-
live in the memories of the past, and every aspect of
bygone service, occupying the mind with solemn reality,
should become the inspiration of a prayer to heaven.
Men had better not break away from their work, than
spend the interval in idleness, or in unholy temper ; far
better would it be for them to continue in Nineveh,
where they would have no time for indolent reverie, or
peevish protest against a kindly Providence.

*Jonah anxiously waited with an earnest desire that the
toil in Nineveh should end in harmony with his preconceived
wish.*   As we have said, there was no great harm in his
going out of the city, in his eastward position, or even
in his building the booth, had it all been done in a prayerful spirit ; but every movement in relation to his depar-
ture from Nineveh was rendered sinful by the petulant
manner in which he seeks to gratify his own pride, to
the eternal ruin of a vast nation.   Had he been re-
signed to the will and Providence of God, his waiting
would have been a triumph, instead of a defeat; it
would have been a token of power, instead of a sign of
weakness.

While in the waiting attitude we cannot but observe
the helpless condition in which the Prophet appears to us.
He is out of harmony with the good of his fellows ; he
is out of sympathy with the Providence of God. Could
any artist sketch a truer picture of utter helplessness

than this. Jonah is in deep anxiety, with nothing but
an angry spirit to keep him company. He cannot conquer himself. He has no power with God as once he
had. He has nothing to afford him comfort. He is
away from his friends. He is unpitied. The past is
a disappointment. The future is a constant dread to
him. Thus we see that an angry, self-willed man, is the
most helpless sight in the world, and nowhere is this
rendered more evident than in the narrative before us.

And the Lord God prepared a gourd, and made it to come up over
Jonah, that it might be a shadow over his head, to deliver him from
his grief. So Jonah was exceeding glad of the gourd.—*Verse 6.*

The subject of this verse is *the ameliorating influences of human life.* Whether we regard the life of
Jonah, with its disobedience, weariness, and pain, or
that of society at large, we cannot but acknowledge
that human life needs a soothing influence to hush its
cry of grief. Contemplate *the pain consequent upon the
commercial toil of men.* What anxiety fills the hearts
of multitudes of our business men as they wend their
way in a morning to their usual place of toil. What
labour have they to expend in order to gain a daily
livelihood. Nor does their anxiety, their effort, end
with one little period of time, but is too frequently the
heritage of a whole life. Think also of *the pain consequent upon the social relationships of life.* One friend
deceives another and the agony of a shattered friendship is experienced. Death enters the home and carries
therefrom the one on whom all its hopes and joys were
centred. The social relationships of life are wires on
which unnumbered messages of grief are flashed into

our hearts.   And other sources of pain might be
narrated, but these abundantly indicate that kindly influences are needed to mitigate the sorrow of life. These
ameliorating influences are of two kinds :—

*Those procured through the effort and contrivance of
man.* The narrative informs us that Jonah made a booth
to shade him from the heat. So when the scorching rays
of pain strike fiercely upon the human heart, man has
the ability to contrive for himself some means of relief.
When his secular matters occasion anxiety, and enforce
strenuous efforts, he frequently obtains shelter in a booth
of his own construction.   He can change his situation.
He can undertake a new enterprise.   Or if his social
relationships are the occasion of pain, there are many
remedial influences at his disposal, in which he can take
refuge.   *The hope of remuneration has an ameliorating
effect upon the pain of commercial life.*   True, man may
be anxious about his secular achievements, he may
labour to render them happy and effective, and in so
doing he is cheered by the thought of expected remuneration. Or perhaps that one day the vexation of his
work will be removed by the repose and enjoyment of
fortune. *The love of the domestic relationships of life
has an ameliorating effect upon the pain of society.*
After the crash and ruin of life, abroad in the wide
world, how calm is the repose of the home.   And even
when the family itself is wounded by grief, how inspiring are the words and looks of the little child,
whose smile is as the balm of Gilead to her father's
troubled heart.   Also *education has an ameliorating influence upon the pain of society.* If society were entirely
ignorant, its pain would be much more intense than

now. But its partial enlightenment tends to calm its passion, refine its thought, direct its impulse, and subserve its effort for the highest good of the race. The information gained by a study of science, history, and the general principles of life, has thus a mitigating effect upon the grief of the world. Many of these booths man can build for himself; he can by care and effort attain to commercial prosperity, and enjoy domestic peace, whereby the anxiety and unrest of his daily life may be effectually removed. But there are other and more effective influences that mitigate the pain of human life.

Those given by the kindly mercy of God. "And the Lord God prepared a gourd, and made it to come up over Jonah, that it might be a shadow over his head, to deliver him from his grief." While wealth, education, and friends tend much to relieve the poverty, ignorance and loneliness of life, there are higher and truer blessings by which they are solaced and enriched, truly Divine in their origin. *There are the abiding consolations of religion.* Though the man may be weary, though the sun may be fierce, yet there is the gourd of true piety to inspire his exhausted energies, and to avert the scorching rays. Religion is the great shading influence of human life, and but for its kindly shelter, we should be in constant torture. *There is the word of inspired truth.* This is a gourd which God has made to grow up over man, to protect him from trial and suffering. What would be the mental uncertainty, and the moral agony of the race if it were but withered up. The Bible is the gourd under which the entire world can take refuge from its sorrow and doubt. *There are the influences of the Divine Spirit.* These are available to our wearied natures, and mitigate more than anything else the pain of human life. The Holy Spirit of God is ever near to the human heart, to remove its burden, to dry its tears, and to inspire it with hope.

These gourds are the immediate gift of God to the human race, and are far more welcome than the booths of our own contrivance. " So Jonah was exceeding glad of the gourd." No doubt he was pleased with the comfort afforded by his own booth, but the narrative would seem to indicate that he was especially thankful for the growth of the gourd. It was far superior to anything he himself had made. Hence his subsequent grief at its loss. And no booths that we can extemporise afford such shelter as our Divinely given gourds. Wealth may be even more trying than poverty, knowledge may be more injurious than ignorance, even love may but shapen the arrow of pain, but the consolations of religion are incapable of anything but our essential good. Just leave the world for one day, to take shelter under the booths of its own construction, and it would soon be exceeding glad of the growth of the gourd. *We should be careful to take a proper advantage of these ameliorating influences of life.* Not to use the God-given gourd merely for our comfort, but also for our moral improvement and instruction. If Jonah had not prayed under his own *booth*, he ought to have done so immediately upon the growth of the gourd. The gifts of God should inspire us with the thought of Himself, and His claims upon our attention and devotion.

But God prepared a worm when the morning rose the next day, and it smote the gourd that it withered.—*Verse 7.*

While in the last verse we had a comparison between the gourd and the ameliorating influences of human life, in this verse we have a contrast between the two.

We are taught here, *that the ameliorating influences of human life are entirely subject to the Divine control.* As God had given the gourd to Jonah, so He removed it after it had afforded him but a temporary comfort. So all the gourds that give relief to life are liable to perish. Our knowledge may be stricken by insanity. Our wealth may be wasted in a panic. Our loves may be dissolved in death. And, after years of impenitent conduct, the consolations of religion may be withdrawn. The Bible may cease to charm our souls, and the Holy Spirit may leave us without the hope of mercy. All the shadows that cool and refresh us are entirely at the Divine command. But there is also a great contrast between the withering of the gourd and the Divinely given influences that mitigate the grief of life. The gourd may wither and die, while to the good and prayerful, the consolations of piety are eternal as their Author. They are always in lovely bloom, to spread a kindly shelter over a contrite heart.

We find here *that the ameliorating influences of human life are sometimes removed at the most unlikely and unexpected times.* It withered in the morning. We should have thought that the light of the returning day would have quickened it into new energy and beauty, whereas it witnessed its decay. So in the morning of our life, when least expected, our wealth has become deepest want, our knowledge the truest ignorance, and our spiritual consolations have been removed through our lack of continuance in the right. God can wither our gourds, our choicest gifts, at the very moment when we expect them to flourish, and when we most need their shelter.

We see here *the power of a little instrumentality to destroy the chief comfort of a human life.* It was a worm that destroyed the gourd of the Prophet. So it does not require great agencies to wither up our hopes and joys. The most trivial ailment may shroud our homes in the darkness of death. The smallest incident of change in the commercial world may dispel all our dreams of luxury and fortune. One little sin may remove our trust in God, and take away the rich comfort of His Spirit. Thus the Divine Being has all the destructive agencies of the material world at His command, and employs them for the discipline of human souls that, appealing to them through their temporal sources, He may gain the more earnest heed. Yes, even the destroying influences of life are commissioned by God. He can destroy a gourd as well as cause one to grow, and if we rejoice in the gifts of life to the exclusion of the giver, the worm is sure to be sent that they may wither in the morning.

And it came to pass, when the sun did arise, that God prepared a vehement east wind; and the sun beat upon the head of Jonah, that he fainted, and wished in himself to die, and said, It is better for me to die than to live.—*Verse* 8.

In this verse *we have exemplified the conduct of some good people under affliction.* Jonah is now passing through severe trial. His gourd is withered; and the

heat of the sun, and the piercing wind are rendered
more fierce than usual by the special interference of
God. Thus we find *that the afflictions that come upon
men are Divinely commissioned.* " God prepared a
vehement east wind." Very likely the Prophet would
not see in this terrible wind any indication of the
Divine intervention. He would possibly regard it as a
natural occurrence, without reference to his own personal condition and character. Men, and especially
when they are in an unholy temper, are very slow to
recognise the Divine hand in their afflictions. We
ought ever to remember that trials spring not up out of
the dust, but being the result of the Divine wishes,
are intended to accomplish a holy purpose.

*The afflictions that come upon men are often very
severe.* " A vehement east wind." It would almost
appear as if the life of Jonah was to be one of continued suffering and perplexity. He has had but a
narrow escape from death before, and here he is again
exposed to rough elements that seem likely to end his life.
And how many times has a vehement east wind swept
across our lives with terrible effect, blasting all our
dearest hopes. There is the east wind of commercial
failure, of social calumny and reproach, and especially
of the providential dispensations of God. These winds
have many times howled about us, and we have been
almost without shelter from their fury. *The afflictions
that come upon men are often complicated.* There was
not only the vehement east " wind," but there was also
the " sun " beating fiercely upon the head of Jonah.
So it does sometimes happen that God allows trials to
come in a crowd upon our lives. Let us then remember

that He is too wise to err, and too good to be unkind.
*The afflictions that come upon men often happen at
the most inopportune time.* The east wind came upon
Jonah when he had lost his gourd, and consequently
when he was entirely without a refuge from the storm.
So it often happens, that the trials of life overtake
individuals and families at the most inopportune
times, when any power to mitigate their grief is entirely
beyond command. It is this that makes the grief
so intense ; the thought that the very gourd that could
have afforded us relief has only a few moments ago
perished, and left us shelterless. One trial is often
preparatory to another ; the withering up of the gourd
is frequently the herald of the vehement east wind.
The discipline of life advances from stage to stage till
its great purpose is accomplished.

*These afflictions have often a most exhaustive effect
upon those to whom they come.* "That he fainted." We
can hardly wonder, after the time he had waited with
but scanty shelter, after the little repose he would be
able to gain owing to the disquiet of his mind, after the
vehement east wind and the scorching sun, that he
should fall to the ground utterly exhausted. Had he
not been a moderately strong man he would have
fainted before this, after such continuous labours in the
wicked Nineveh. So trial has a most exhausting effect
upon many around us. If you go into many homes in
the city you will see pale faces, wan countenances, and
almost skeleton forms ; and if you ask the meaning of
such prostration, the answer will be found in some sick
relative, or in some mental anxiety beyond the ken of the
outside world. Nothing has such an exhaustive effect

upon the human frame as sorrow. Many lives are worn into the grave by it.

These afflictions often occasion a complaining spirit. "It is better for me to die than to live." The scorching sun, the keen east wind, and his withered gourd, made Jonah dissatisfied with life, and rather than continue existence under such conditions he would die. And there are no doubt many fervent souls of great trial, who long for the grave, where the heat of the sun never penetrates, and where the keen east wind is unknown. Trial generally tends to make men dissatisfied with life, but it is well for those who can bear it in an uncomplaining spirit, knowing that it is of Divine appointment, designed for their eternal good.

And God said to Jonah, Doest thou well to be angry for the gourd? And he said, I do well to be angry, even unto death.— *Verse* 9.

In this verse *we get the first glimpse into the meaning of the discipline exercised toward Jonah.* The Divine intention was not to fix the attention of Jonah on the east wind, but on the gourd, which gave him such joy, and whose removal he regretted. And now we see that the Lord had by His recent dealings with the Prophet been laying down the premise of an argument, by which He should convince him of the inconsistency of his conduct in relation to Nineveh. We cannot but remark *how kindly the Divine discipline was exercised towards Jonah.* There is a touch of pity in the verse, as though the Divine Being felt that in the removal of the gourd Jonah had sustained a great loss, with which he sympathized. The discipline of God towards us is generally merciful, though we may think otherwise. True the burning sun and the fierce wind do not seem to have much of kindness in them, but the first voice that speaks to our souls after they have ceased to injure us, is one of tenderest compassion. *The discipline toward Jonah was instructive.* The gourd was not arbitrarily removed from him. The east wind was not the result of caprice. The heat did not strike on him merely to occasion pain. The purpose of this severe discipline was to instruct his soul. He needed to be Divinely taught in reference to the future of Nineveh, and in these last few verses we see him in the school of heaven, learning a lesson he is very slow to comprehend. *The discipline toward Jonah was progressive.* The Divine discipline toward the Prophet did not disclose its meaning and its intention all at once. At first it would seem to have no connection with the moral condition of his life. The gourd would not appear to have any relation to his Nineveh mission; and instead of being the emblem of severity, its welcome shelter would appear the token of kindness. But step by step the discipline proceeds and unfolds its intention, until the gourd gives place to the wind and sun. This is typical of the Divine dealings with us. There are links (often unseen) connecting all our trials, and making them into one harmonious discipline for our good.

We see here *how man unconsciously enhances the forcefulness of the Divine discipline.* "And he said, I do well to be angry, even unto death." Thus Jonah himself admits the premise of the Divine argument, so that when it is applied to Nineveh, he has no way to escape its conclusion. It is very likely that the Prophet did not invest the east wind and the sun with any moral significance, and unthinkingly responded to the Divine enquiry. Be this as it may, the very admission of Jonah was the foundation of the Divine appeal to him in reference to the reprieved crowds of Nineveh. So it is with us now, we often reply to Divine interrogation in such a manner that we enhance our own conviction, and proclaim the justice and wisdom of that Providence against which we have been so long contending.

Then said the Lord, Thou hast had pity on the gourd, for the which thou hast not laboured, neither madest it grow ; which came up in a night, and perished in a night.—*Verse* 10.

We see in this verse *the inconsistency which sometimes characterises the conduct of good men.* " Thou hast had pity on the *gourd.*" Jonah was exceedingly glad when the green plant was given to shelter him from the wind and heat, and deeply regretted its removal, yet when the Divine Being, in the royalty of His mercy, wished to save a vast city from destruction, the Prophet was angry. How self-contradictory was his conduct. He lamented the withering of the plant because his own safety was endangered. He regarded his own welfare with far greater anxiety than the moral good of Nineveh. Surely we should have imagined that the man who would mourn the loss of a plant, would with far deeper feeling lament the destruction of a city. But no, a selfish disposition makes a man contradict himself, and especially invites the Divine discipline. Frequently God appeals to such by a removal of their temporary comforts, that he may inspire within them the power of a disinterested sympathy. He takes away their gourds that He may teach them pity and charity, two of the most important lessons a human spirit can learn. It is by this severe correction, that many men are rendered self-forgetful and self-harmonious.

The inconsistency of Jonah's conduct is seen in *that the gourd was not endeared to him by the experiences of labour on its behalf.* "For the which thou hast not laboured, neither madest it to grow." When men have spent their mental or bodily energy in the production or contrivance of any desired object, they generally feel a kind of regard for it, deep in proportion to the purpose it serves, or the toil that has been necessary for its completion. Labour creates a sort of unspoken relationship between the object made, and he whose skill has made it. The artist is very truly related to his picture. It is the offspring of his mind and genius. It is the reproduction of his inner soul. The sculptor lingers over the statue, carving it into beauty, until it almost speaks to him, and his admiration for it, when completed, is indicative of something more than a mere proprietorship. And the more fatiguing the labour, the more painful the work, the truer is the sympathy and relationship created thereby. The deepest intimacies of life are the offspring of pain. It is instinctive to man to love anything that has cost him mental agony, or bodily exhaustion. These are the most valuable coins of his nature, and render aught purchased thereby most precious. But Jonah had not toiled for this gourd. He had experienced no pain in its production. He felt not toward it the kinship of a workman who had made it. It was given to his exhausted frame even without his request; yet he regarded its removal with deep pity. If then his commiseration was excited by the withering of a paltry plant, surely he ought to have rejoiced at the gourd of Divine mercy that was now spreading its benign shade over the doomed crowds of repentant Nineveh. Why should he wish it to be withdrawn? He is indeed a contradiction to himself.

Further, the inconsistency of Jonah's conduct is seen in *that the gourd was not endeared to him by its long continuance*. " Which came up in a night, and perished in a night." Very often we find that time has an endearing tendency. It renders valuable many things otherwise of but small intrinsic worth. They are sacred because they remind us of a buried past. The first time that we see an object of beauty we experience a momentary thrill of joy, but a longer acquaintance therewith discovers new glories, and renders the old ones more familiar to us; hence every day adds new value to what had at first but the charm of novelty. There is a pathos in the flight of time to which the human heart is very sensitive. And age makes a much more tender affinity appear to the soul of man than mere novelty. But Jonah's gourd had not thus been endeared to him, for it came up in a night, and perished in a night. He had only a temporary enjoyment of its shade, and but a short contemplation of its beauty. But the gourd of Divine mercy, now spreading over Nineveh, would be an eternal shelter to the multitudes whose reformed character would happily repose in the forgiving love of God. Every day they would see new beauty in it, and enter into richer experiences of its benefit. And thus Jonah regretting the removal of a plant that had given him a momentary shade, ought to have had sympathy with the reprieve of Nineveh, which would be to that city an eternal shelter. Again we cannot but see how self-contradictory was his conduct. He was capable of a tender feeling, but its wave of sympathy rarely reached to other hearts; its whole force was spent upon himself, and yielded but little comfort. That man is the happiest whose tide of pity flows, like the sea to the shore, to the whole human race, so that it not merely breaks upon himself, but also upon the crowds in Nineveh.

> And should not I spare Nineveh, that great city, wherein are more than six score thousand persons that cannot discern between their right hand and their left hand; and also much cattle?—*Verse* 11.

In this verse God terminates his controversy with Jonah, and, it would seem from the silence of the narrative, leaves him humbled and ashamed. The Prophet was convinced of his folly, could say nothing to excuse it, and so the history ends. Had he replied to the Divine argument, it would probably have been recorded as before. Very likely he has come to a better state of mind again.

Hence the Divine Being asserts his right to spare Nineveh. "And shall not *I* spare Nineveh." Here the Divine Being places Himself in contrast with Jonah —"*Thou* hast had pity on the gourd." "Thou," a frail creature of limited sympathies, of feeble insight into the purposes of heaven. "Thou hadst pity on the gourd, and shall not I spare Nineveh." Consider two or three reasons why the Divine Being should spare this city.

Because He is the sovereign Ruler of the universe. God had a right to save Nineveh after her reformation of character. He is sovereign in the exercise of His mercy, and no one can stay or question the propriety of its outflow to the penitent. What right, then, had Jonah to place himself in antagonism to the Divine will in this respect, or suspect the propriety of the Divine procedure. Truly it is better to fall into the hands of God, than even into the hands of many of His Prophets. Let us never contend with the sovereign mercy of the Infinite; to do so is man's pride and ruin.

Because He is in truest sympathy with the moral good of men. It was for the good of Nineveh that her life should be prolonged. By this arrangement she would be enabled to develope the new principles now implanted within her heart, and she would also have opportunity of manifesting, to surrounding nations, the beauty and power of her reformed character. And thus Nineveh, instead of preaching a gospel of ruin, would speak from her strong battlements a more emphatic message of hope and peace. Nineveh standing would proclaim a more inviting gospel than Nineveh destroyed. Thus the Divine Being, as the truest friend of man, naturally desired to save the imperilled multitudes. Nor had Jonah any reason now to suspect the mercy of the Divine intention.

Jonah ought to have acquiesced in the Divine wish, because the salvation of Nineveh was of the highest importance. " And shall not I spare *Nineveh*." Nineveh is here contrasted with the gourd given to Jonah, under the shelter of which he rejoiced. Nineveh was a city of immortal souls; the gourd was only a perishing plant whose destiny was the dust. The gourd was one by itself, whereas in the city there were crowds of people. Surely then if Jonah lamented the former, he ought with far greater reason to have mourned the destruction of the latter. Thus, the Divine Being shows to Jonah, the folly and inconsistency of his peevish temper. The Divine idea of salvation is the truest and the best. Though we cannot always enter into its rich meaning, yet let us never question its rectitude.

Contemplate *the pathos of this argument.* "Wherein are more than six score thousand persons that cannot discern between their right hand and their left hand; and also much cattle." Thus the children of Nineveh are made an argument for her reprieve. God estimates a city, not by the prowess of its army, the wealth of its commerce, the learning of its academies, the splendour of its high society, but by the number of its children. There is a great power in young life to avert calamities, and invite the favour of heaven. We little know the benedictions that flow out upon the world through the lives of the little, gladsome ones around us.

We have now finished our contemplations on this Book. *Let us not think too harshly of Jonah.* Probably this narrative is only one scene in his life, and that the most unworthy of his entire career. As it would not be right to pass an opinion on a book after only reading one chapter, on a musical composition after only playing one bar, on a painting after only studying one of its aspects, so it would not be right to condemn the entire life of Jonah by the petulant disposition manifested by him on this occasion. It was not probably the natural habit of his mind, but may only have been called forth by the trying circumstances of his mission to Nineveh. Let us therefore be as charitable to him as we can.

Some may ask why this Book was written? Was it written merely to shew the perversity of one man in a certain crisis of his life? Was it penned as the sketch of a romantic life? No! Its intention was to fore-shadow in many respects the life and work of our Lord Jesus Christ, both by comparison and contrast. As light is seen in the poorest picture, so a Christ to come into the relations of human life gleams through the wonderful pages of Jonah's history. Jonah's three days' residence in the sea, and subsequent deliverance therefrom, were a type of Christ's death and resurrection from the grave; and his preaching to Nineveh, and its salvation was typical of Pentecost, and awaits yet its full significance in the final subjugation of all men to the Saviour. Let us pray that all nations may imitate the example of the heathen city, and turn to God with full purpose of heart.